Word Recognition and Meaning Vocabulary: A Literacy Skills Primer

Paul C. Burns
Late of University of Tennessee at Knoxville

Betty D. Roe
Tennessee Technological University

Elinor P. Ross
Tennessee Technological University

Houghton Mifflin Company
Boston   New York

*Dedicated to Michael H. Roe
and James R. Ross*

Sponsoring Editor: Loretta Wolozin
Associate Editor: Lisa Mafrici
Associate Project Editor: Amy Johnson
Senior Production/Design Coordinator: Carol Merrigan
Senior Manufacturing Coordinator: Sally Culler

Cover Designer: Rebecca Fagan
Cover Image: Copyright Joanne Dugan/Graphistock

Library of Congress Catalog Card Number: 98-73648

ISBN: 0-395-93972-0

123456789-DC-02 01 00 99 98

Contents

Meaning Vocabulary   68

Introduction

This primer is a concise, yet thorough, guide to word recognition skills and vocabulary development. It is meant to supplement texts that lack complete coverage of these topics, or to stand alone as a source of information for the elementary literacy educator. It covers not only skills and content, but also includes activities and instructional procedures for applying these skills.

With new emphasis being placed on the importance of teaching word recognition skills and vocabulary, this primer should serve the needs of many educators. It is for the classroom teacher who is seeking ideas for instructional activities that are consistent with current best practice. It is also a convenient, focused source of information on phonics generalizations and terminology for the preservice teacher who is learning to teach reading, as well as for the inservice teacher who wants a review or some fresh ideas for teaching. For the administrator, evaluator, or staff developer, it is a convenient reference guide, and for the resource or Title 1 teacher it provides a quick, efficient way to locate skills and find appropriate instructional procedures.

This introduction contains a general overview of the importance of reading and continues with a presentation of twelve basic principles for teaching reading, to provide the foundation upon which the primer is based. Part I of the primer focuses on word recognition, specifically sight words, context clues, phonics, structural analysis, and dictionary study. Phonics receives extensive treatment with attention given to terminology, generalizations, and applications. Sample plans offer ideas for teaching different types of phonics lessons. Part II presents information on meaning vocabulary, beginning with general information on vocabulary development and instruction. Its primary emphasis is on instructional procedures, which include practical, high-interest activities for motivating students to increase their vocabularies. This part features the use of context clues, structural analysis, and various forms of graphic organizers.

Throughout this primer, model activities suggest ideas for applying generalizations and strategies. In addition, the "Classroom Scenario" feature takes the reader inside the classroom to see how instructional procedures are actually implemented, and "Focus on Strategies" gives a realistic portrayal of how selected strategies may be used. "Time for Reflection" allows the reader to pause periodically and reflect on the meaning of the preceding content. With their realistic, thought-provoking nature, these special features help the reader become aware of effective ways to teach word recognition and meaning vocabulary.

The Importance of Reading

The ability to read is vital to functioning effectively in a literate society such as ours. However, children who do not understand the importance of learning to read will not be motivated to learn. Learning to read takes effort, and children who see the value of reading in their personal activities will be more likely to work hard than those who fail to see the benefits.

Teachers should have little trouble demonstrating to children that reading is important. Every aspect of life involves reading. Road signs direct travelers to particular destinations, inform drivers of hazards, and remind people about traffic regulations. There are menus in restaurants, labels on cans, printed advertisements, newspapers, magazines, insurance forms, income tax forms, and campaign and travel brochures. These reading situations are inescapable. Even very young children can be helped to see the need to read the signs on restrooms, the labels on individual desks in their classrooms, and the labeled areas for supplies. In fact, these young children are often eager to learn to read and are ready to attack the task enthusiastically. However, children do not automatically realize the "profusion of literacy activities in the nonschool world" (Kotrla, 1997, p. 702).

Reading tasks become increasingly complex as students advance through the grades and require continuing improvement. Anderson (1988) suggests sparking the interest of middle grade students through career education activities, helping them in this way to see that reading is a life skill that is relevant to their future success. The children can choose occupations that interest them and list the reading skills each occupation requires. They can take one or more field trips to businesses to see workers using reading to carry out their jobs, and they can hear resource people speak to their classes about how they personally need reading in their jobs. These resource people may bring to class examples of the reading materials they must use to perform their daily tasks. The students may also interview parents and others to learn about reading demands in a wide variety of careers. In many cases, the reading activities involve such applications as use of computer databases and electronic mail.

As important as functional reading is to everyday living, another important goal of reading is enjoyment. Teachers must attempt to show students that reading can be interesting to them for reasons other than strictly utilitarian ones. Students may read for relaxation, vicarious adventure, or aesthetic pleasure as they immerse themselves in tales of other times and places or those of the here and now. They may also read to obtain information about areas of interest or hobbies to fill their leisure time. To help children see reading as a pleasurable activity,

Students may read for relaxation, vicarious adventure, or aesthetic pleasure, as well as to gain information. (© *Laimute E. Druskis/Stock Boston*)

teachers should read to them each day on a variety of themes and topics, from a variety of genres, and from the works of many authors. They should also make many books available for children to look at and read for themselves, and they should set aside time for children to read from self-selected materials. Students should be given opportunities to share information from and reactions to their reading in both oral and written forms. They should be encouraged to think about the things they are reading and to relate them to their own experiences.

Twelve Principles of Teaching Reading

Principles of teaching reading are generalizations about reading instruction based on research in the field of reading and observation of reading practices. The principles listed here are not all-inclusive; many other useful generalizations about teaching reading have been made in the past and will continue to be made in the future. They are, however, the ones we believe are most useful in guiding teachers in planning reading instruction.

Principle 1   Reading is a complex act with many factors that must be considered.

The reading process has nine aspects: sensory, perceptual, sequential (linear, logical, and grammatical patterns), experiential, thinking, learning, associational (sounds and symbols, words and meanings), affective (interests, attitudes, and self concepts), and constructive.

Principle 2   Reading involves the construction of the meaning represented by the printed symbols.

A person who fails to derive meaning from a passage has not been reading, even if he or she has pronounced every word correctly. "In addition to obtaining information from the letters and words in a text, reading involves selecting and using knowledge about people, places, and things, and knowledge about texts and their organization. A text is not so much a vessel containing meaning as it is a source of partial information that enables the reader to use already-possessed knowledge to determine the intended meaning" (Anderson et al., 1985, p. 8).

Readers construct the meanings of passages by using both the information conveyed by the text and their prior knowledge, which is based on their past experiences. Obviously, different readers construct meaning in somewhat different ways because of their varied experiential backgrounds. Some readers do not have enough background knowledge to understand a text; others fail to make good use of the knowledge they have (Anderson et al., 1985). For example, suppose a text mentions how mountains can isolate a group of people living in them. Students familiar with mountainous areas will picture steep grades and rough terrain, which make road building difficult, and will understand the source of the isolation, although the text never mentions it. Affective factors, such as the reader's attitudes toward the subject matter, also influence the construction of meaning, as does the context in which the reading takes place.

Principle 3   There is no one correct way to teach reading.

Some methods of teaching reading work better for some children than for others. Each child is an individual who learns in his or her own way. Some children are visual learners; some are auditory learners; some are kinesthetic learners. Some need to be instructed through a combination of modalities, or avenues of perception, in order to learn. The teacher should differentiate instruction to fit the diverse needs of the students. Of course, some methods also work better for some teachers than they do for others. Teachers need to be acquainted with a variety of methods, including ones that involve technology, so that they can help all of their students.

Principle 4   Learning to read is a continuing process.

Children learn to read over a long period of time, acquiring more advanced reading skills after they master prerequisite skills. Even after they have been introduced to all reading skills, the process of refinement continues. No matter how old they are or how long they have been out of school, readers continue to refine their reading skills. Reading skills require practice. If readers do not practice, the skills deteriorate; if they do practice, their skills continue to develop.

Principle 5 Students should be taught word recognition strategies that will allow them to unlock the pronunciations and meanings of unfamiliar words independently.

Children cannot memorize all the words they will meet in print. Therefore, they need to learn techniques for figuring out unfamiliar words so that they can read when the assistance of a teacher, parent, or friend is not available.

Principle 6 The teacher should assess each student's reading ability and use the assessment as a basis for planning instruction.

Teaching all children the same reading lessons and hoping to deal at one time or another with all the difficulties students encounter is a shotgun approach and should be avoided. Such an approach wastes the time of those children who have attained the skills currently being emphasized and may never meet some of the desperate needs of other children. Teachers can avoid this approach by using assessment instruments and techniques to pinpoint the strengths and weaknesses of each child in the classroom. Then they can either divide the children into needs groups for pertinent instruction or give each child individual instruction.

Principle 7 Reading and the other language arts are closely interrelated.

Reading—the interaction between a reader and written language through which the reader tries to reconstruct the writer's message—is closely related to the other major language arts (listening, speaking, and writing). Learning to read should be treated as an extension of the process of learning spoken language, a process that generally takes place in the home with little difficulty if children are given normal language input and feedback on their efforts to use language.

A special relationship exists between listening and reading, which are *receptive* phases of language, as opposed to the *expressive* phases of speaking and writing. Mastering listening skills is important in learning to read, for direct association of sound, meaning, and word form must be established from the start. The ability to identify sounds heard at the beginning, middle, or end of a word and the ability to discriminate among sounds are essential to successful phonetic analysis of words. Listening skills also contribute to the interpretation of reading material.

Students' listening comprehension is generally superior to their reading comprehension in the elementary school years. Although reading and listening are not identical and each has its own advantages, they are alike in many ways. For example, both are constructive processes. In reading, the reader constructs the message from a printed source with the help of background knowledge; in listening, the listener constructs the message from a spoken source with the help of that same background knowledge.

People learn to speak before they learn to read and write. Children's reading vocabularies generally consist largely of words in their oral language (listening and speaking) vocabularies. These are words for which they have previously developed concepts and, thus, can comprehend.

Speaking, like the other language arts, is a constructive process. The speaker puts together words in an attempt to convey ideas to one or more listeners. The reader works at constructing meaning from the words the writer has put on paper.

The connection between reading and writing is particularly strong. First, both reading and writing are basically constructive processes. Readers must construct or attempt to reconstruct the message behind a written text. Readers evaluate the accuracy of their message construction as they monitor their reading processes; they may revise the constructed meaning if the need is apparent.

Starting with purposes for writing that affect the choice of ideas and the way these ideas are expressed, writers work to create written messages for others to read. In completing the writing task, they draw on their past experiences and their knowledge of writing conventions. As they work, they tend to read and review their material in order to evaluate its effectiveness and to revise it, if necessary.

The strategies and skills needed for the language arts are interrelated. For example, the need to develop and expand concepts and vocabulary, which is essential to reading, is evident in the entire language arts curriculum. Concepts and vocabulary terms to express these concepts are basic to listening, speaking, and writing as well as to reading activities. Spoken and written messages are organized around main ideas and supporting details, and people listen and read to identify the main ideas and supporting details conveyed in the material.

Principle 8   Using complete literature selections in the reading program is important.

Students need to experience the reading of whole stories and books to develop their reading skills. Reading isolated words, sentences, and paragraphs does not give them the opportunity to use their knowledge of language and story structure to the fullest, and reading overly simplified language both reduces the opportunities to use their language expertise *and* dampens interest in reading the material. Whole pieces of literature can include students' own writing and the writing of other children as well as the works of commercial authors.

Principle 9   Reading is an integral part of all content area instruction within the educational program.

Teachers must consider the relationship of reading to other subjects within the curriculum of the elementary school. Frequently other curricular areas provide applications for the skills taught in the reading period. Textbooks in the various content areas are often the main means of conveying content concepts to students. Supplementary reading of library materials, magazines, and newspapers is also frequently used. Inability to read these materials with comprehension can

Reading can be an enjoyable pursuit.
(© *Laimute E. Druskis/ Stock Boston*)

mean failure to master important ideas in science, mathematics, social studies, and other areas of the curriculum. Students who have poor reading skills may therefore face failure in other areas of study because of the large amount of reading these areas often require. In addition, the need to write reports in social studies, science, health, or other areas can involve many reading and study skills: locating information; organizing information; and using the library and multimedia reference sources, including the Internet.

Teachers who give reading and writing instruction only within isolated periods and treat reading and writing as separate from the rest of the curriculum will probably experience frustration rather than achieve student change and growth. Although a definite period scheduled specifically for language instruction (listening, speaking, reading, and writing) may be recommended, this does not mean that teachers should ignore these areas when teaching content subjects. The ideal situation at any level is not "reading" and "writing" for separate time periods, followed by "study" of social science or science for the next period. Instead, although the emphasis shifts, language learning and studying should be integrated during all periods at all levels.

Principle 10   The student needs to see that reading can be an enjoyable pursuit.

It is possible for our schools to produce capable readers who do not read; in fact, today this is a common occurrence. Reading can be entertaining as well as informative. Teachers can help students realize this fact by reading stories and poems to them daily and setting aside a regular time for pleasure reading, during which many good books of appropriate levels and from many interest areas are readily available. Teachers can show children that reading is a good recreational pursuit by describing the pleasure they personally derive from reading in their spare time and by reading for pleasure in the children's presence. When the children read recreationally, the teacher should do this also, thereby modeling desired behavior. Pressures of tests and reports should not be a part of recreational reading times. Students in literature-based reading instructional programs that include self-selection of reading materials and group discussion of chosen reading materials are likely to discover the enjoyable aspects of reading for themselves.

Principle 11   Reading should be taught in a way that allows each child to experience success.

The stage of the child's literacy development should be considered for all instructional activities throughout the grades. Not only when reading and writing instruction begins, but whenever instruction in any language strategy takes place, at all grade levels, teachers should consider each child's readiness for the instructional activity. If the child's literacy development is not adequate for the task, the teacher should adjust the instruction so that it is congruent with the student's literacy level. This may involve instruction to provide a child with readiness to incorporate the new learning into his or her store of concepts.

Asking children to try to learn to read from materials that are too difficult for them ensures that a large number will fail. Teachers should give children instruction at their own levels of achievement, regardless of grade placement. Success generates success. If children are given a reading task at which they can succeed, they gain the confidence to attack the other reading tasks they must perform in a positive way. This greatly increases the likelihood of their success at these later tasks. In addition, some studies have shown that if a teacher *expects* students to be successful readers, they will in fact *be* successful.

Teachers tend to place poor readers in materials that are too hard for them more frequently than they place good readers in such materials. Children who are given difficult material to read use active, comprehension-seeking behaviors less often than do children who are reading material they can understand with a teacher's assistance. Placing poor readers on levels that are too high tends to reinforce the inefficient reading strategies that emerge when material is too difficult, making it less likely that these readers will develop more efficient strategies. Although they do not have high expectations of success under any circumstances, their expectations of success decrease more after failure than do those of good readers (Bristow, 1985).

Teachers should place poor readers in material they can read without undue focus on word recognition. This approach allows poor readers to focus on comprehending the text. Poor readers must be convinced that they will gain greater understanding during reading if they apply strategies they have learned (Bristow, 1985).

Asking children to read from materials that do not relate to their backgrounds or experiences can also result in less successful experiences. In view of the wide cultural diversity found in schools today, teachers must be particularly sensitive to this problem and must provide relevant materials for children that offer them a chance for success.

Principle 12   *Encouragement of self-direction and self-monitoring of reading is important.*

Good readers direct their own reading, making decisions about how to approach particular passages, what reading speed is appropriate, and *why* they are reading the passages. They are able to decide when they are having difficulties with understanding and can take steps to remedy their misunderstandings (Anderson et al., 1985). When they do this, they are using metacognitive strategies.

No matter what teaching approaches are used in a school or what patterns of organization predominate, these principles of teaching reading should apply. Each teacher should consider carefully his or her adherence or lack of adherence to such principles.

In order to implement many of these principles, teachers need to understand specific skills and be able to use them appropriately for instructional purposes. We will now look specifically at *Part I: Word Recognition*, which deals directly with word recognition skills that children need to become independent readers.

I

Word Recognition

SETTING OBJECTIVES

When you finish reading Part I, you should be able to

▶ Describe some ways to help a child develop a sight vocabulary.

▶ Describe some activities for teaching use of context clues.

▶ Discuss the role of phonics in the reading program.

▶ Define each of the following terms: *consonant blend, consonant digraph, vowel digraph, diphthong.*

▶ Describe how to teach a child to associate a specific sound with a specific letter or group of letters.

▶ Discuss ways to teach the various facets of structural analysis.

▶ Identify the skills children need in order to use a dictionary as an aid in word recognition.

Pay close attention to these terms when they appear in this primer.

analytic approach to
  phonics instruction

cloze procedure

context clues

homographs

inflectional endings

onset

phonemic awareness

phonics

rime

semantic clues

sight words

structural analysis

syntactic clues

synthetic approach to
  phonics instruciton

word configuration

In addition, pay close attention to the specific phonics terms discussed in Part I.

Part I Organization

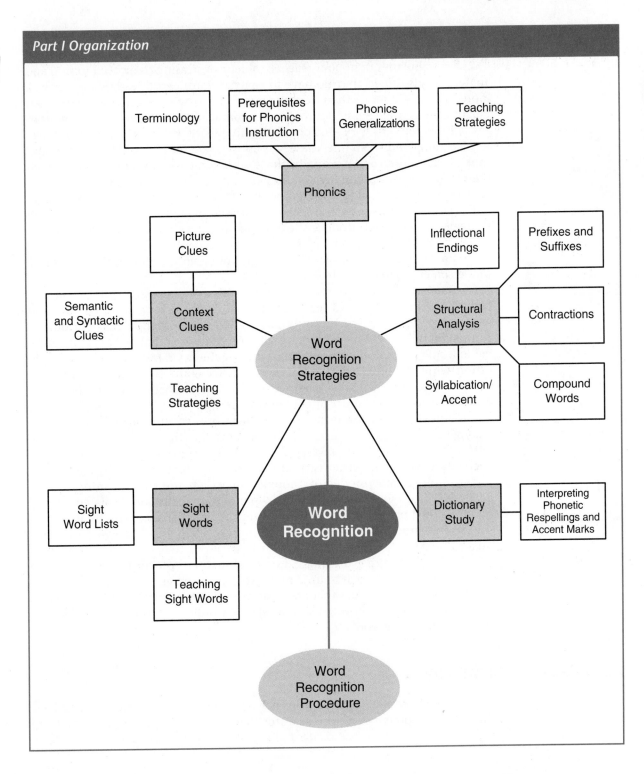

Good readers differ from poor readers in both the size of sight vocabularies and the ability to decode words. Good readers tend to have larger sight vocabularies than poor readers, thereby decreasing their need to stop and analyze words. When they do have to analyze words, good readers often have a more flexible approach than poor readers do because they generally have been taught several strategies and have been encouraged to try a new one if one strategy fails (Jenkins et al., 1980). Poor readers frequently know only a single strategy for decoding words. No one strategy is appropriate for all words, however, and thus these children are at a disadvantage when they encounter words for which their strategy is not useful. Even if they have been taught several strategies, poor readers may have failed to learn a procedure that will allow them to decode unfamiliar words as efficiently as possible. "Research suggests that, no matter which strategies are used to introduce them to reading, the children who earn the best scores on reading comprehension tests in the second grade are the ones who made the most progress in fast and accurate word identification in the first grade" (Anderson et al., 1985, pp. 10–11).

Samuels (1988) sees word recognition skills as "a necessary prerequisite for comprehension and skilled reading" and points out that "we need a balanced reading program, one which combines decoding skills and the skills of reading in context" (pp. 757, 758). He has long supported the idea that accurate and automatic word recognition is necessary for reading fluency. This automaticity (application without conscious thought) in word recognition is achieved through extended practice. Repeated readings of the same passages can help move students from accuracy to automaticity in word recognition.

Adams (1991) also endorses the need for word recognition skills along with strategies for acquiring meaning. She encourages "thorough overlearning of letters, spelling patterns, and spelling-sound correspondences—and also of vocabulary, syntactic patterns, rhetorical devices, text structures, conceptual underpinnings, and modes of thought on which the full meaning of text depends." However, she denounces "'ponderous drills' on 'isolated skills'" (Adams, 1991, p. 394). She also emphasizes the need for automaticity in decoding to free students' attention for comprehension ("A Talk with Marilyn Adams," 1991).

Part I of this primer presents a variety of methods of word recognition and stresses a flexible approach to unfamiliar words, encouraging application of those word recognition strategies that are most helpful at the moment. It also explains ways to show children how to use a number of word recognition strategies jointly to help in decoding words.

Word Recognition Strategies

Word recognition strategies and skills help a reader recognize written words. They include development of a store of words that can be recognized immediately on sight and the ability to use context clues, phonics, structural analysis, and dictionaries for word identification where each strategy is appropriate. The last four types are sometimes referred to as *word attack* strategies or skills.

Children need to be able to perform all of the word recognition strategies because some will be more helpful than others in certain situations. Teaching a single approach to word identification is not wise, because children may be left without the proper tools for specific situations. In addition, depending on their individual abilities, children find some word recognition strategies easier to learn than others. A child who has a hearing loss, for example, may not become very skillful at using phonics but may learn sight words easily and profit greatly from the use of context clues.

Instruction in word recognition should not dominate reading time. Much time should be spent in reading connected text; Stahl (1992) suggests half of the time or more. Attention to comprehension instruction should also receive ample time.

Gill (1992, p. 450) warns that instruction in word recognition "hinders progress when it places the child in reading material on his frustration level," because this prevents the child from extracting information from patterns that he or she is capable of detecting in the text. When children are taught with materials that emphasize repetitions of spelling patterns, they tend to develop strategies based on alphabetic principles. To accomplish this, they need to be exposed to texts that contain unchanging patterns that they are able to detect. Some children also need assistance in detecting these patterns.

Sight Words

Young readers also need to develop a store of sight words, words that are recognized immediately without having to resort to analysis. The larger the store of sight words a reader has, the more rapidly and fluently he or she can read a selection. Comprehension and reading speed suffer if a reader has to pause too often to analyze unfamiliar words. The more mature and experienced a reader becomes, the larger his or her store of sight words becomes. (Most, if not all, of the words used in this textbook, for example, are a part of the sight vocabularies of college students.) Thus, one goal of reading instruction is to turn all the words students continuously need to recognize in print into sight words.

Artley (1996) suggests development of a basic stock of sight words first, then teaching of other methods of word recognition. This allows inductive reasoning about sound-symbol associations and other word elements, such as prefixes and suffixes. There are a number of reasons why sight words need to be taught:

1. The English language contains a multitude of irregularly spelled words, that is, words that are not spelled the way they sound. Many of these are among the most frequently used words in our language. The spellings of the following common words are highly irregular in their sound-symbol associations: *of, through, two, know, give, come,* and *once.* Rather than trying in vain to sound out these words, children need to learn to recognize them on sight as whole configurations.

Young readers need to develop a store of sight words. (© *David Young Wolff/Photo Edit*)

2. Learning several sight words at the very beginning of reading instruction gives the child a chance to engage in a successful reading experience very early and consequently promotes a positive attitude toward reading.

3. Words have meaning for youngsters by the time they arrive at school, but single letters have no meaning for them. Therefore, presenting children with whole words at the beginning allows them to associate reading with meaning rather than with meaningless memorization.

4. After children have built up a small store of sight words, the teacher can begin phonics instruction with an analytic approach. (More about the analytic approach appears later in Part I.)

Most children know some sight words when they first come to school. They have learned the names of some of their favorite fast-food restaurants and other businesses from signs, the names of some of their favorite foods and drinks from the packages or labels, or both categories of words, as well as others, from television commercials. Children who have been read stories while sitting on their parents' laps may well have picked up vocabulary from favorite stories that were repeatedly shared. Still, the sight vocabularies of beginning students are meager compared to those mature readers need.

A teacher must carefully choose which words to teach as sight words. Extremely common irregularly spelled words (*come, to, two*) and frequently used regularly spelled words (*at, it, and, am, go*) should be taught as sight words so that children can read connected sentences early in the program. The first sight words should be useful and meaningful. A child's name should be one of those words; days of the week, months of the year, and names of school subjects are other prime candidates. Words that stand for concepts unfamiliar to youngsters are poor choices. Before children learn *democracy* as a sight word, for example, they need to understand what a democracy is; therefore, this is not a good word to teach in the primary grades.

Teaching some words with regular spelling patterns as sight words is consistent with the beliefs of linguists who have become involved in developing reading materials. Words with regular spelling patterns are also a good base for teaching "word families" in phonics; the *an* family, for example, includes *ban, can, Dan, fan, man, Nan, pan, ran, tan,* and *van*.

Sight Word Lists

Lists of basic sight words may give teachers an indication of the words that are most frequently used in reading materials and therefore needed most frequently by students. The Dolch list of the 220 most common words in reading materials (excluding nouns), though first published in the 1930s, has repeatedly been found to be relevant and useful in more recent materials (Mangieri and Kahn, 1977; Palmer, 1985). Another well-known list of basic sight words is Fry's "Instant Words" (Fry, 1977). This list presents the words most frequently used in reading materials.

Teaching Sight Words

Before children begin to learn sight words, they must have developed visual discrimination skills; that is, they must be able to see likenesses and differences among printed words. It is also helpful, although not essential, for them to know the names of the letters of the alphabet, because this facilitates discussion of likenesses and differences among words. For example, a teacher could point out that, whereas *take* has a *k* before the *e, tale* has an *l* in the same position.

A potential sight word must initially be identified for learners. A teacher should show the children the printed word as he or she pronounces it, or pair the word with an identifying picture. Reading aloud to children as they follow along in the book is one way to identify vocabulary for children within a meaningful context. Regardless of the method of presentation, one factor is of paramount importance: the children must *look* at the printed word when it is identified in order to associate the letter configuration with the spoken word or picture. If children fail to look at the word when it is pronounced, they have no chance of remembering it when they next encounter it.

Teachers should also encourage children to pay attention to the details of the word by asking them to notice ascending letters (such as *b, d, h*), descending letters (such as *p, g, q*), word length, and particular letter combinations (such as double letters). Careful scrutiny of words can greatly aid retention.

The most natural, holistic approach to sight word instruction is reading to children as they follow along. Teachers may use this approach with groups of students when big books are available, allowing all children in the group to see the words. They may also read from books that are available in multiple copies in the classroom, with each child or pair of children following along on his or her own copy of the story. Books with accompanying tapes or records can promote sight vocabulary in a similar way.

Children learn early to recognize some sight words by their visual *configurations,* or shapes. Teachers should not overly stress this technique, because many words have similar shapes. But since many children seem to use the technique in the early stages of reading, regardless of the teacher's methods, a teacher can use configuration judiciously to develop early sight words. One way to call attention to shape is to have the children frame the words to be learned:

The limitation of configuration as a sight word recognition clue is demonstrated by the following words:

Teachers can call attention to word makeup through comparison and contrast, comparing a new word to a similar known word: *fan* may be compared to *can* if the children already have *can* in their sight vocabularies. Either the teacher can point out that the initial letters of the words are different and the other letters are the same, or the students can discover this on their own. The latter method is preferable, because the students are likely to remember their own discoveries longer than they will remember something the teacher has told them.

Few words are learned after a single presentation, although Ashton-Warner (1963) claims that children will instantly learn words that are extremely important to them. Generally, a number of repetitions are necessary before a word actually becomes a sight word.

Veatch (1996) asserts that Aston-Warner's Key Vocabulary approach, in which children pick words that have intense meaning for them, is efficient and reliable in developing sight vocabulary. The teacher writes on cards the words the children choose and gives them to the children. The children say the letters in the words, trace them (moving left to right), and use the words (to write stories, to play games, and so on).

The teacher should carefully plan practice with potential sight words. This practice should be varied and interesting, because children will more readily learn those things that interest them. Games are useful if they emphasize the words being learned rather than the rules of the game.

Practice with potential sight words should generally involve using the words *in context*. Children cannot pronounce many words out of context with certainty—for example, *read*. The following sentences indicate the importance of context:

I *read* that book yesterday.   I can't *read* without glasses.

Another reason for using context when presenting sight words is that many commonly used words have little meaning when they stand alone. Prime examples are *the, a,* and *an*. Context for words may be a sentence (*The* girl ate *a* pear and *an* apple.) or short phrases (*the* girl, *a* pear, *an* apple). Context is also useful if pronunciation is less clear than it should be. Children may confuse the word *thing* with *think* unless the teacher has presented context for the word: "I haven't done a useful thing all day."

McGill-Franzen (1993) points out the value of highly predictable books, such as those used in the Reading Recovery Program, for beginning readers. Peterson (1991) has arranged a continuum of Reading Recovery books from easy to more complex, based partially on the context provided. The books at the easiest levels are highly predictable from the pictures and repetitive sentence patterns. Saccardi (1996) also recommends the use of predictable books for many literacy activities and suggests particular books and appropriate uses for each.

The language experience approach, in which students' own language is written down and used as the basis for their reading material, is good for developing sight vocabulary. This approach provides a meaningful context for learning sight words, and it can be used productively with individuals or groups. The word-bank activities associated with this approach are particularly helpful.

Teachers may also present words in conjunction with pictures or with the actual objects the words name, such as chairs and tables, calling attention to the fact that the labels name the items. These names can be written on the board so that youngsters can try to locate the items in the room by finding the matching labels.

Constructing picture dictionaries, in which children illustrate words and file the labeled pictures alphabetically in a notebook, is a good activity for helping younger children develop sight vocabulary. This procedure has been effective in helping children whose primary language is not English learn to read and understand English words.

Teachers can use labels to help children learn to recognize their own names and the names of some of their classmates. On the first day of school, the teacher can give each child a name tag and label each child's desk with his or her name.

The teacher may also label the area where the child is supposed to hang a coat or store supplies. The teacher should explain to the children that the letters written on the name tags, desks, and storage areas spell their own names and that no one else is supposed to use these areas. The children should be encouraged to look at the names carefully and try to remember them when locating their belongings. Although the children may initially use the name tags to match the labels on the desks and storage areas, by the time the name tags are worn out or lost, the children should be able to identify their printed names without assistance.

The teacher can generally accelerate this process by teaching children how to write their names. Children may first trace the name labels on their desks with their fingers. Next, they can try to copy the names on sheets of paper. At first, the teacher should label all students' work and drawings with the students' names, but as soon as the children are capable of writing their names, they should label their own papers. From the beginning, the children's names should be written in capital and lower-case letters, rather than all capitals, since this is the way names most commonly appear in print.

The days of the week can also be taught as sight words. Each morning, the teacher can write "Today is" on the chalkboard and fill in the name of the appropriate day. At first the teacher may read the sentence to the children at the beginning of each day, but soon some children will be able to read the sentence successfully without help.

Function words—words, such as *the* and *or,* that have only syntactic meaning rather than concrete content—are often particularly difficult for children to learn because they lack concrete meaning and because many of them are similar in physical features. These words need to be presented in context repeatedly so that the surrounding words can provide meaning (Hargis et al., 1988). Jolly (1981) suggests teaching these troublesome words by presenting only one word at a time of a pair of words that are likely to be confused (for example, *was* and *saw*). He also suggests teaching words with more obvious differences in features first, then those with subtler differences. For example, teach *that* with words like *for* and *is* before presenting it with *this* and *the*. Teachers can also delete the words from passages, leaving blanks for the students to fill in with the target words.

Much teaching of sight word recognition takes place as a part of basal reader lessons. The teacher frequently introduces the new words, possibly in one of the ways discussed here, before reading, discussing meanings at the same time. Then students have a guided silent reading period during which they read material containing the new words in order to answer questions asked by the teacher. Purposeful oral rereading activities offer another chance to use the new words. Afterward, teachers generally provide practice activities suggested in the teacher's manual of the basal reading series. Follow-up activities may include skill sheets, games, manipulative devices, and special audiovisual materials. Writing new words is helpful for some learners, especially for kinesthetic learners (those who learn through muscle movement).

Games such as word bingo are useful for practice with sight words. The teacher or a leader calls out a word, and the children who recognize that word on their cards cover it. When a child covers an entire card, he or she says, "Cover," and the teacher or leader checks the card to see if all the covered words were actually called.

Another technique is to list sight words on a circular piece of cardboard and have children paper-clip pictures to appropriate words. The teacher can make this activity self-scoring by printing the matching words on the backs of the pictures, as shown here.

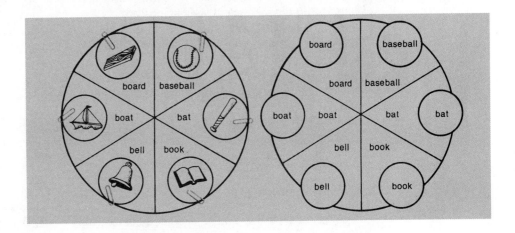

Dickerson (1982) compared the use of physically active games, passive games, and worksheets in an attempt to discover which would be most effective in increasing the sight vocabularies of remedial first graders. The physically active games proved to be most effective, followed by the passive games. Worksheets were the least effective, although the children who used the worksheets did gain some sight vocabulary. Teachers may consider increasing use of more active games, such as those in which children stand and act out action verbs. The Classroom Scenario that follows describes such an activity.

Classroom Scenario

Developing Sight Vocabulary

Mr. Barkley, a first-grade teacher, found that three children were having trouble remembering the action words in the stories they were reading. He called these children over to a corner of the room near the chalkboard and wrote these words on the board: *jump, walk, run.* He introduced the words by saying, "We have seen these words in our stories this week, but they have been hard for you to remember, so we are going to practice reading them as we play a game. This word is *jump.* Can you jump for me?" The children jumped. Then he said, "Good. Whenever you read the word *jump* for this game, I want you to jump just like that."

(continued)

Mr. Barkley introduced *walk* and *run* in the same way. The students readily demonstrated each one.

Then Mr. Barkley brought out a board game with a racetrack oval drawn on it. Each space in the path around the oval had a simple sentence containing either *jump, walk,* or *run* written on it. The children took turns spinning a spinner and moving the number of spaces indicated around the racetrack with a personally selected token (one of several different miniature race cars). A child who landed on a space had to read the sentence, tell what it meant, and perform the action in the sentence. For example, the child might read, "Mary can jump," and then say, "That means Mary can do this." Then the child would stand up and jump. If a child could not read the sentence or tell/show what it meant, another player could "steal his or her play" by reading the sentence and performing the action. The player who got to try this would be determined by having the opponents of the player who missed spin the spinner for a high number.

The first child around the track won the game, but all three children were actively involved with the action words and made progress in reading them correctly as the game continued.

Analysis of Scenario

Mr. Barkley used a physically active game to develop the children's sight vocabularies after more passive reading activities had failed to be effective with these children. He targeted the activity for the children who were having difficulty, not forcing the repetitive practice on those who had mastered the words. He presented the words in sentence contexts to encourage children to recognize the words in typical reading situations, rather than as isolated entities.

Ceprano (1981) reviewed research on methods of teaching sight words and found that no one method alone was best for every student. She found evidence that teaching the distinctive features of words helped children learn. She also found evidence that use of picture clues along with specific instruction to focus attention on the words facilitated learning. She reported, however, that some research indicates that teaching words in isolation or with pictures does not ensure the ability to read words in context. In fact, indications are that "most learners need directed experience with written context while learning words in order to perceive that reading is a language process and a meaning-getting process" (p. 321). Therefore, when teachers are working with sight-word instruction, it seems wise to present words in context rather than just in isolation.

| **Time for Reflection** | Some people believe sight words should be taught in context. Others believe they should be taught in isolation. **What do *you* think?** |

Context Clues

Context clues—the words, phrases, and sentences surrounding the words to be de-coded—help readers determine what the unfamiliar words are. Here we will focus on the function of context clues as *word recognition* aids.

The teacher should carefully plan practice with potential sight words. (© *Tony Freeman/ Photo Edit*)

Since research has found that syntactic and semantic context influence readers' identification of words, it is important that word recognition skills be introduced and practiced in context (Jones, 1982). Much of the written material to which primary-level readers are introduced falls well within their comprehension as far as vocabulary and ideas are concerned, but these youngsters cannot always recognize in printed form the words that are familiar in oral form. Context clues can be extremely helpful in this process. Research also shows that context clues help younger and poorer readers recognize words more than they help older and better readers (Gough, 1984; Daneman, 1991).

Picture Clues

Picture clues are generally the earliest context clues children use. If children are exposed to many pictures of a character, such as one named Julie, in beginning reading materials, they may come to recognize the character instantly. When they are shown a page containing a picture of Julie and a single word, they may naturally assume that the word names the picture and that the word is *Julie*. If they do not relate the picture to the word in this manner, the teacher can ask a question such as "Who is in the picture?" to lead them toward understanding the relationship. If a child responds, "A girl," the teacher might ask, "What kind of letter is at the beginning of the word?" The response "A capital letter" would prompt the question "What kinds of words have we talked about that begin with capital letters?" After eliciting the answer "Names," the teacher can then ask, "What is the name of the girl in the picture?" This question should produce the response "Julie." Finally, the teacher asks, "Now what do you think the word is?" At this point, a correct response is extremely likely. The teacher should use a procedure that encourages the use of picture clues *along with,* rather than apart from, the clues available in the printed word.

Teachers should not overemphasize picture clues. These clues may be useful in the initial stages of instruction, but they become less useful as the child advances to more difficult material, which has a decreasing number of pictures and an increasing proportion of print. Encouraging too much reliance on pictures may result in too little time spent on developing word analysis skills.

Semantic and Syntactic Clues

As soon as possible, teachers should encourage first-grade children to use written context as a clue to unknown words. The idea of using context clues can be introduced by oral activities like the following Model Activity. The sentences can often be drawn from stories that have just been read or listened to in class.

In the sample sentences in the Model Activity, children can use both semantic (meaning) and syntactic (grammar) clues in choosing words to fill in the blanks. Youngsters generally use these two types of clues in combination, but to clarify their differences, we will consider them separately first.

Semantic clues are clues derived from the meanings of the words, phrases, and sentences surrounding the unknown word. In the examples just given, children

Use of Oral Context

Model Activities

Read sentences such as the following to the children, leaving out words as indicated by the blanks. Sentences can be drawn from books the teacher plans to share later in class. After reading each sentence, ask the children what word they could use to finish the sentence in a way that would make sense. The children will find that the sentences that have missing words at the end are easier. In some cases, the children may suggest several possibilities, all of which are appropriate. Accept all of these contributions with positive comments.

Sample sentences:

1. Jane went out to walk her _____ .
2. John was at home reading a _____ .
3. They were fighting like cats and _____ .
4. I want toast and _____ for breakfast.
5. Will you _____ football with me?

can ask themselves the following questions to decide what words would make sense:

Sentence 1. What are things that can be walked?

Sentence 2. What are things that can be read?

Sentence 3. What expression do I know about fighting that has *like cats and* in it?

Sentence 4. What food might be eaten with toast for breakfast?

Sentence 5. What things can you do with a football?

Various kinds of semantic clues exist, including the following:

1. *Definition clues.* A word may be directly defined in the context. If the child knows the word in oral form, he or she can recognize it in print through the definition.

   The *dictionary* is a book in which the meanings of words can be found.

2. *Appositive clues.* An appositive may offer a synonym or a description of the word that will cue its recognition. Children need to be taught that an appositive is a word or phrase that restates or identifies the word or expression it follows and that it is usually set off by commas, dashes, or parentheses.

   They are going to *harvest,* or gather in, the season's crops.

   That model is *obsolete* (outdated).

   The *rodents*—rats and mice—in the experiment learned to run a maze.

3. *Comparison clues.* A comparison of the unfamiliar word with a word the child knows may offer a clue. In the examples, the familiar words *sleepy* and *clothes* provide the clues for *drowsy* and *habit.*

Like her sleepy brother, Mary felt *drowsy.*

Like all the clothes she wore, her riding *habit* was very fashionable.

4. *Contrast clues.* A contrast of the unknown word with a familiar one may offer a clue. In the examples, the unfamiliar word *temporary* is contrasted with the familiar word *forever,* and the unfamiliar word *occasionally* is contrasted with the familiar word *regularly.*

It will not last forever; it is only *temporary.*

She doesn't visit regularly; she just comes by *occasionally.*

5. *Common-expression clues.* Familiarity with the word order in many commonly heard expressions, particularly figurative expressions, can lead children to the identity of an unknown word. In the context activity discussed earlier, children needed to know the expression "fighting like cats and dogs" to complete the sentence. Children with varied language backgrounds are more likely to be able to use figurative expressions to aid word recognition than are children with less developed backgrounds.

He was as quiet as a *mouse.*

Daryl charged around like a bull in a *china* shop.

6. *Example clues.* Sometimes examples are given for words that may be unfamiliar in print, and these examples can provide the clues needed for identification.

Mark was going to talk about *reptiles*—for example, snakes and lizards.

Andrea wants to play a *percussion* instrument, such as the snare drum or the bells.

Syntactic clues are provided by the grammar or syntax of our language. Certain types of words appear in certain positions in spoken English sentences. Thus, word order can give readers clues to the identity of an unfamiliar word. Because most children in schools in the United States have been speaking English since they were preschoolers, they have a feeling for the grammar or syntax of the language. Syntactic clues help them discover that the missing words in sentences 1 through 4 in the oral-context activity presented earlier in this section are nouns, or naming words, and that the missing word in sentence 5 is a verb, or action word.

Looking at each item, we see that in sentence 1 *her* is usually followed by a noun. *A* is usually followed by a singular noun, as in sentence 2. Sentences 3 and 4 both employ *and,* which usually connects words of the same type. In sentence 3, children are likely to insert a plural animal name because of the absence of an article (*a, an, the*). Similarly, in sentence 4 *and* will signal insertion of another food. Sentence 5 has the verb marker *will,* which is often found in the sequence "Will you (verb) . . . ?"

As we pointed out earlier, semantic and syntactic clues should be used *together* to unlock unknown words.

Teaching Strategies

Early exercises with context clues may resemble the oral-context exercise explained earlier. It is good practice for a teacher to introduce a new word in context and let children try to identify it, rather than simply telling them what the word is. Then children can use any phonics and structural analysis knowledge they have, along with context clues, to help them identify the word. The teacher should use a context in which the only unfamiliar word is the new word; for example, use the sentence "My *umbrella* keeps me from getting wet when it rains" to present the word *umbrella*. The children will thus have graphic examples of the value of context clues in identifying unfamiliar words.

When a child encounters an unfamiliar word when reading orally to the teacher, instead of supplying the word, the teacher can encourage the child to skip it for the time being and read on to the end of the sentence (or even to the next sentence) to see what word would make sense. The teacher can encourage use of the sound of the initial letter or cluster of letters, sounds of other letters in the word, or known structural components, along with context. In a sentence where *hurled* appears as an unknown word in the phrase *hurled the ball,* a child might guess *held* from the context. The teacher could encourage this child to notice the letters *ur* and try a word that contains those sounds and makes sense in the context. Of course, this approach will be effective only if the child knows the meaning of *hurled*. Encouraging the child to read subsequent sentences could also be helpful, since these sentences might disclose situations in which *held* would be inappropriate but *hurled* would fit.

A cloze passage, in which words have been systematically deleted and replaced with blanks of uniform length, can be a good way to work on context clue use. For this purpose, the teacher may delete certain types of words (nouns, verbs, adjectives, etc.) rather than using random deletion. The students should discuss their reasons for choosing the words to be inserted in the blanks, and the teacher should accept synonyms and sometimes nonsynonyms for which the students have a good rationale. The point of the exercise is to have the students think logically about what makes sense in the context.

Use of context clues can help children make educated guesses about the identities of unfamiliar words. Context clues are best used with phonics and structural analysis skills because they help identify words more quickly than phonics or structural analysis clues alone would. But without the confirmation of phonics and structural analysis, context clues provide only guesses. As we mentioned earlier, when a blank is substituted for a word in a sentence, students can often use several possibilities to complete the sentence and still have it make sense. When children encounter unknown words, they should make educated guesses based on the context and verify those guesses by using other word analysis skills.

A modified cloze procedure can be used with a story summary to develop children's skill in decoding in a meaningful context. The first letter of the deleted word is provided, helping children use their knowledge of sound-symbol relationships as well as choosing words that make sense in the context (Johnson and Louis, 1987).

DeSerres (1990) introduces basal reader stories' mastery vocabulary by presenting each word on the board in sentence context, having students write the word in another sentence or phrase context on 3" × 5" word cards for their word banks, and letting them share their sentences. Later she uses modified cloze stories (in which selected words, rather than regularly spaced words, are deleted) with the mastery words as the words chosen for omission. Students fill in the blanks by choosing from their word cards as the class reads the story together. Then they fill in the blanks on individual copies of the stories and read them to partners. Partners point out parts that do not make sense. Later, students produce their own stories. This procedure gives practice with using context.

A child who encountered the following sentence with a blank instead of a word at the end might fill in the blank with either *bat* or *glove*:

> Frank said, "If I am going to play Little League baseball this year, I need a new ball and _____ ."

If the sentence indicated the initial sound of the missing word by presenting the initial letter *g,* the child would know that *glove,* rather than *bat,* was the appropriate word.

> Frank said, "If I am going to play Little League baseball this year, I need a new ball and g_____ ."

Structural analysis clues can be used in the same way. In the following sentence, a child might insert such words as *stop* or *keep* in the blank.

> I wouldn't want to _____ you from going on the trip.

The child who had the help of the familiar prefix *pre-* to guide his or her choice would choose neither. The word *prevent* would obviously be the proper choice.

> I wouldn't want to pre_____ you from going on the trip.

Suffixes and ending sounds are also very useful in conjunction with context to help in word identification. Teachers can use exercises similar to the following to encourage children to use phonics and structural analysis clues along with context clues. Sample sentences can be drawn from stories that the children are about to read in class.

Model Activities

Word Identification

Write the following sentences on the board.

1. This package is too h _ _ _ y for me. Let someone else carry it.

2. I want to join the Navy and ride in a sub _ _ _ _ _ _ .

3. If you keep up that arguing, you will sp _ _ _ the party for everyone.

4. You can't hurt it. It's <u>in</u> _ _ <u>str</u> _ _ _ <u>ible</u>.

5. She lives in a <u>pent</u> _ _ _ _ _ apartment.

6. My grandmother has a home <u>r</u> _ _ _ <u>dy</u> for any disease.

Ask the children to read the sentences silently and to try to identify the incomplete words from the clues in the surrounding words and the letters or groups of letters that have been supplied. Let volunteers go to the board and complete the incomplete words. Ask these volunteers if they can tell how the clues in the sentences helped them decide on the words to write. Encourage the students to use the same strategy to figure out other unfamiliar words in the story they are about to read.

Some words are difficult to pronounce unless they appear in context. *Homographs*—words that look alike but have different meanings and pronunciations, such as *row, wind, bow, read, content, rebel, minute, lead, record,* and *live*—are prime examples. Here are some sentences that demonstrate how context can clarify the pronunciations of such words:

1. The *wind* is blowing through the trees.
   Did you *wind* the clock last night?

2. She put a *bow* on the gift.
   You should *bow* to the audience when you finish your act.

3. Would you *rebel* against that law?
   I have always thought you were a *rebel.*

4. Did your father *record* his gas mileage?
   Suzanne broke Jill's *record* for the highest score in one game.

Although most of the examples in this section show only a single sentence as the context, children should be encouraged to look for clues in surrounding sentences as well as in the sentence in which the word occurs. Sometimes an entire paragraph will be useful in defining a term.

Phonics

Before you read this section, go to "Test Yourself" at the end of Part I and take the multiple-choice phonics test. It will give you an idea of your present knowledge of phonics. After you study the text, go back and take the test again to see what you have learned.

Phonics is the association of speech sounds (*phonemes*) with printed symbols (*graphemes*). In some languages, this sound-symbol association is fairly regular, but not in English. A single letter or combination of letters in our alphabet may stand for many different sounds. For example, the letter *a* in each of the following words has a different sound: *cape, cat, car, father, soda.* On the other hand, a single sound may be represented by more than one letter or combination of letters. The long *e* sound is spelled differently in each of the following words: *me, mien, meal, seed,* and *seize.* To complicate matters further, the English language abounds with words that contain letters that stand for no sound, as in is*l*and, k*n*ig*h*t, *w*rite, lam*b*, *g*nome, *p*salm, and r*h*yme.

The existence of these spelling inconsistencies does not imply that phonics is not useful in helping children decode written English. We discuss inconsistencies to counteract the feeling of some teachers that phonics is an infallible guide to pronouncing words in written materials. Teaching phonics does not constitute a complete reading program; rather, phonics is a valuable aid to word recognition when used in conjunction with other skills, but it is only *one* useful skill among many. Mastering this skill, with the resulting ability to pronounce most unfamiliar words, should not be considered the primary goal of a reading program. Children can pronounce words without understanding them, and deriving *meaning* from the printed page should be the objective of all reading instruction.

Groff (1986) found that, if beginning readers can attain an approximate pronunciation of a written word by applying phonics generalizations, they can go on to infer the true pronunciation of the word. He found, for example, that "100% of the second graders tested could infer and produce the *o* of *from* as /u/ after first hearing it as /o/. The pronunciation /from/ was close enough to /frum/ for these young pupils to infer its correct pronunciation" (p. 921). Groff concluded that children need practice in making such inferences. First, they need to apply phonics generalizations to unfamiliar words, producing approximate pronunciations of the words. Then they can infer the real pronunciations of the words by thinking of words they know that are close in sound to the approximations achieved by the generalizations.

Skilled readers appear to identify unfamiliar words by finding similarities with known words (Anderson et al., 1985). For example, a reader might work out the pronunciation of the unknown word *lore* by comparing it with the known word *sore* and applying the knowledge of the sound of *l* in other known words, such as *lamp*. Cunningham (1978, 1979) suggests using a similar approach to identify polysyllabic words as well as single-syllable words.

Carnine (1977) studied the transfer effects of phonics and whole word approaches to reading instruction and found superior transfer to new words among the students who were taught phonics. The phonics group even had greater transfer to irregular words, although it was not extensive. Research with adults has been interpreted as indicating that teachers should present *several* sound-symbol correspondences for each grapheme rather than one-to-one correspondences, thereby providing their students with a set for diversity. If such a procedure had been used in this study, it might have produced more transfer to irregular words.

Phonics techniques are not intended to be ends in themselves; rather, they are means to the end of successful reading. Maclean (1988) sees phonics as "a catalyst which triggers the process of learning to read" (p. 517). It helps students pair spoken and written words and lays the groundwork for them to develop their own decoding routines, which may bear little resemblance to the rules used in phonics instruction. In order for the phonics catalyst to produce a reaction, children must be allowed to do large amounts of reading in appropriate materials.

The following Classroom Scenario shows one way that phonics principles begin to form in classes.

Classroom Scenario

Development of Phonics Knowledge

Marty, a first grader, was turning the pages of a calendar in his classroom, finding numbers that he recognized on each page. Suddenly he called to his teacher excitedly, "Mrs. Overholt, this is almost like my name!"

Mrs. Overholt joined Marty at his table. "Yes, it is," she replied. "Show me the part that is the same."

Marty pointed to the letters *M, a, r,* in sequence.

"That's right," Mrs. Overholt said. "Can you tell me what month this is?"

"No," Marty said.

"The month is March," said Mrs. Overholt. "Does it sound a little like your name, too?"

"Yes," Marty almost squealed. "The beginning of it sounds like the beginning of my name."

"You really listened carefully to hear that," Mrs. Overholt said. "Those letters stand for the same sounds in your name and in the word *March.* Keep your eyes open for other words like this. You may be able to figure out what they are by remembering what you found out about letters and sounds."

Analysis of Scenario

Mrs. Overholt used a teachable moment with Marty. He had made a discovery about words that excited him and his teacher helped him to expand it.

A good phonics program provides sufficient reinforcement for a skill that is being taught and offers a variety of reinforcement opportunities (Spiegel, 1990). The practice activities in this text offer some ideas for reinforcement opportunities. Although reinforcement in phonics instruction may include practice with single letters and sounds, it must include application of the strategy or skill with whole words and longer pieces of discourse, such as sentences and paragraphs. Spiegel (1990) suggests the following sequence: "auditory discrimination of the sound of interest, visual discrimination of the letter pattern, and then work with words, sentences, and short paragraphs" (p. 328). We believe this practice should be expanded to include work with whole selections, such as predictable books that contain the letter-sound association that is being emphasized. In fact, a whole selection, in the form of a big book, may be shared with the children orally, with children chiming in on the highly predictable parts wherever possible. From this beginning, the teacher may have students locate the letter representing the sound under consideration, listen for the sound as he or she reads portions of the story aloud again, and make their own generalizations about the relationship between the sound and the letter that represents it. The children will not state their personal generalizations in the same form as the rules that would be found in a reading text, but they will understand the connection more deeply and retain it better if they have discovered it themselves.

Morrow and Tracey (1997) found that preschool teachers often used context-based phonics instruction (teaching letter-sound associations in meaningful or functional contexts), whereas kindergarten, first-grade, and second-grade teachers used more explicit phonics instruction (sequential, systematic presentation of sound-symbol associations, employing direct instructional strategies in isolation from meaningful contexts). Few teachers at any of these levels used an approach that combined explicit instruction and context-based instruction, an approach that appears to have much merit. Lapp and Flood (1997) point out that when children are taught language skills and strategies in a context that includes the exploration of books, a balanced approach to literacy instruction has been attained.

Time for Reflection	Some people believe children should learn basic skills before they begin reading stories, but others believe they should learn skills as they encounter the need for them within stories. **What do *you* think?**

If students are to learn phonics associations effectively, they need to see a reason for doing so. The relevance of learning sound-symbol associations is much clearer when students can see the letters and sounds as a part of a meaning-bearing system, rather than as isolated bits of meaningless information.

If basal reading series consistently designed the stories and phonics instruction to support each other, the connection between the phonics instruction and achieving meaning when reading might be much clearer. Anderson and others (1985, p. 47) found that "a high proportion of the words in the earliest selections children read should conform to the phonics they have already been taught."

Adams sees the instructional goal of phonics as students' understanding of the alphabetic principle in written English. She points out that participating in language experience activities, writing with invented spelling, sharing books, and reading interesting texts can help in reaching this goal ("A Talk with Marilyn Adams," 1991).

Time for Reflection	Some people think phonics is all that a child needs for a word recognition program. Others think that several different word attack methods are needed. **What do *you* think?**

Terminology

To understand written material about phonics, teachers need to be familiar with the following terms.

Vowels. The letters *a, e, i, o,* and *u* represent vowel sounds, and the letters *w* and *y* take on the characteristics of vowels when they appear in the final position in a word or syllable. The letter *y* also has the characteristics of a vowel in the medial (middle) position in a word or syllable.

Consonants. Letters other than *a, e, i, o,* and *u* generally represent consonant sounds. *W* and *y* have the characteristics of consonants when they appear in the initial position in a word or syllable.

Consonant Blends (or Clusters). Two or more adjacent consonant letters whose sounds are blended together, with each individual sound retaining its identity, constitute a consonant blend. For example, although the first three sounds in the word *strike* are blended smoothly, listeners can detect the separate sounds of *s, t,* and *r* being produced in rapid succession. Other examples are the *fr* in *frame,* the *cl* in *click,* and the *br* in *bread,* to mention only a few. Many teaching materials refer to these letter combinations as consonant clusters rather than consonant blends.

Consonant Digraphs. Two adjacent consonant letters that represent a single speech sound constitute a consonant digraph. For example, *sh* is a consonant digraph in the word *shore* because it represents one sound and not a blend of the sounds of *s* and *h.* Additional examples of consonant digraphs appear on page 37.

Vowel Digraphs. Two adjacent vowel letters that represent a single speech sound constitute a vowel digraph. In the word *foot, oo* is a vowel digraph. Additional examples of vowel digraphs appear on page 38.

Diphthongs. Vowel sounds that are so closely blended that they can be treated as single vowel units for the purposes of word identification are called *diphthongs.* These sounds are actually vowel blends, since the vocal mechanism produces two sounds instead of one, as is the case with vowel digraphs. An example of a diphthong is the *ou* in *out.* Additional examples of diphthongs appear on page 38.

Prerequisites for Phonics Instruction

There seems to be agreement that good auditory and visual discrimination are prerequisites for learning sound-symbol relationships. We know that children must be able to distinguish one letter from another and one sound from another before they can associate a given letter with a given sound. *Visual discrimination* refers to the ability to distinguish likenesses and differences among forms, and *auditory discrimination* refers to the ability to distinguish likenesses and differences among sounds. To achieve these skills, children must first understand the concepts of *like* and *different.* Also, to achieve auditory discrimination, children must have *phonemic awareness,* or the awareness that speech is composed of separate sounds (phonemes). They must be able to hear sounds within words, or they will be unable to form mental connections between sounds and letters (Beck and Juel, 1995; Griffith and Olson, 1992; Juel, 1988, 1991; Ball and Blachman, 1991; Lundberg et al., 1988; Pearson, 1993; Adams, 1990; Gill, 1992). Training in phonemic awareness has been shown to be effective and to have a positive effect on reading acquisition (Lundberg et al., 1988; Yopp, 1992; Bradley and Bryant, 1983). Phonemic awareness activities may ask children "to match words by sounds, isolate a sound in a word, blend individual sounds to form a word, substitute sounds in a word, or segment a word into its constituent sounds" (Yopp, 1992, p. 699). Yopp (1992) points out that playful, gamelike activities such as riddles and guessing games are best because they engage children in the tasks.

Yopp (1995b, p. 20) says, "Most youngsters enter kindergarten lacking phonemic awareness. Indeed, few are conscious that sentences are made up of individual words, let alone that words can be segmented into phonemes." Use of read-aloud books is a way to work on phonemic awareness, because many books have rhyme, alliteration, assonance, and other features that allow children to play with the sounds of language (Yopp, 1995a; Yopp, 1992; Griffith and Olson, 1992).

Richgels, Poremba, and McGee (1996) suggest a "What Can You Show Us?" activity to develop phonemic awareness in a holistic context. They describe it as a "functional, contextualized, social literacy activity" (p. 641). It accompanies shared reading activities. Before shared reading, a *preparation* step involves selecting reading materials and displaying them appropriately; for example, if the text is copied onto a chart, the features in words that the teacher wants to emphasize can be highlighted in some way. The next step involves the children's *previewing* the text and being given a chance to discuss what they see. Next, *student demonstrations* of what they know about the text (for example, identifying letters or words) take place. The shared reading (teacher reading, joint reading, and student activities) comes next. During and after this activity the students apply what they know about the text. There may be further student demonstrations.

Phonemic awareness can be taught directly and may also "develop as a consequence of learning phonics, learning to read, or even learning to write, especially when teachers encourage students to use invented spellings" (Pearson, 1993, p. 507). In whole language classrooms, phonemic awareness and phonics may be learned through invented-spelling activities.

Activities requiring children to discriminate among letter and word forms are more useful to beginning readers than activities requiring them to identify similarities and differences among geometric forms (Sippola, 1985). Unless children need practice in developing the concepts of *like* and *different,* it is pointless to have them make distinctions among shapes and forms. Instead, they need practice with simultaneous and successive visual discrimination of letters and words. Simultaneous discrimination occurs when children match printed symbols that are alike while they can see both symbols. Successive discrimination occurs when children find a duplicate symbol after a stimulus card is no longer visible. Similarly, attention to general sounds in the environment has value only in teaching concepts of *like* and *different* (Sippola, 1985). Beginning readers need to focus primarily on observing similarities and differences in the initial sounds and rhyming sounds of words.

Introducing children to simple rhymes is a good way to sensitize them to the likenesses and differences in verbal sounds. The teacher can ask children to pick out the words that rhyme and to supply words to rhyme with a given word. This ability is fundamental to the construction of "word families." Children should also be able to hear similarities and differences in word endings and in middle vowels; for example, they should be able to tell whether *rub* and *rob*, or *hill* and *pit*, have the same middle sound. Finally, they should be able to listen to the pronunciation of a word sound by sound and mentally fuse or blend the sounds to recognize the intended word.

The following model activities should help children develop visual and auditory discrimination abilities.

Visual Discrimination

Model Activities

Write on the board some letters that are similar in appearance (*b, d,* and *p,* for example) Say to the children: "Let's look at these letters. Are any of them alike? How are the first two letters different? What is different about the other letter?"

Then say to them: "Now I am going to give you a copy of a page of the story that we read today. Look at the first letter on the board. (Point to the letter.) Then look at the page from the story. Every time you see this letter in the story, circle it with your green crayon. (Give them time to search for the letter *b* and mark their pages.) Now look at the second letter. (Point to it.) Every time you see this letter in the story, circle it with your red crayon. (Give them time to do this.) Now look at the third letter. (Point to it.) Every time you see this letter in the story, circle it in yellow. (Give them time to do this.) Then display a large copy of the story and let individuals come up and point to the letters that should have been circled in the different colors, while children check their own papers.

Repeat the activity with a set of words containing these letters, such as *big, pet,* and *dog.* Ask the same questions about the words. Then have the children perform a similar activity with the words, using fresh pages from the story so that their previous marks will not confuse them.

Auditory Discrimination

Model Activities

Name several puppets with double names to stress initial consonant sounds (Molly Mouse, Freddie Frog, Dolly Duck, and Bennie Bear). While holding a puppet, say: "I'd like you to meet Molly Mouse. Molly Mouse only likes things that begin the same way that her name begins. Molly Mouse likes milk, but she doesn't like water. I am going to name some things that Molly Mouse likes or doesn't like. You
(continued)

must listen closely to the way each word begins. Raise your hand if I say something that Molly Mouse likes. Keep your hand down if I say something that Molly Mouse doesn't like. Let's begin. Molly Mouse likes meat." The children should raise their hands. If they don't seem to understand why she likes meat, talk about the beginning sound and give additional examples. Then say: "Molly Mouse likes potatoes." The children should keep their hands down.

Activities

Additional Visual and Auditory Discrimination Activities

Visual Discrimination

1. Locate a page in a big book that has pairs of similar-looking letters close to each other, and help students discover how the letters are alike and how they differ. Examples of letter pairs to use: *d b, p q, m n.*

2. Choose a word that is frequently confused with a similarly shaped word from a big book story that is being shared. Write this word on the board once, along with several repetitions of the word with which it may be confused. Have the children find the word on the board that is different. Then have them locate the same word in the big book story. Read aloud the sentence in which the word appears. Example of words that could be used: *on on no on.*

Auditory Discrimination (beginning sounds)

1. Play a guessing game. Ask if there is anyone in the room whose name starts with the same sound as the beginning of the word *top.* The first child who replies whose name starts with this sound may give the next clue.

2. Find poems that repeat certain sounds. Examples: "Wee Willie Winkie," "Lucy Locket," "Bye-Baby Bunting," "Deedle, Deedle, Dumpling."

Auditory Discrimination (medial and final sounds, whole word)

1. Use riddles to relate sounds to words. For example, ask each child to guess what word, illustrated by the following riddle, begins with the same sound as *pig.*

   I am good to eat.
   I rhyme with *teach.*
   I am a fruit.
   What am I?

2. Let the children supply the missing rhyming word in a familiar verse.

Phonics Generalizations

Some teachers believe that good phonics instruction is merely the presentation of a series of principles that children are expected to internalize and use in the process of word identification. Difficulties arise from this conception, however.

First, pupils tend to internalize a phonics generalization more rapidly and effectively when they can arrive at it inductively. That is, by analyzing words to which a generalization applies and by deriving the generalization themselves from this analysis, children will understand it better and remember it longer.

Second, the irregularity of the English spelling system results in numerous exceptions to phonics generalizations. Children must be helped to see that generalizations help them to derive *probable* pronunciations rather than infallible results. When applying a generalization does not produce a word that makes sense in the context of the material, readers should try other reasonable sound possibilities. For example, in cases where a long vowel sound is likely according to a generalization but results in a nonsense word, the child should be taught to try other sounds, such as the short vowel sound, in the search for the correct pronunciation. Some words are so totally irregular in their spellings that even extreme flexibility in phonic analysis will not produce close approximations of the correct pronunciations. In such situations, the child should be taught to turn to the dictionary for help in word recognition. Further discussion of this approach to word recognition can be found later in Part I.

Third, students can be so deluged with rules that they cannot memorize them all. This procedure may result in their failure to learn any generalization well.

Teachers can enhance a phonics program by presenting judiciously chosen phonics generalizations to youngsters, as long as they are taught, not as unvarying rules, but as guides to best guesses. Authorities vary on which generalizations to present (Bailey, 1967; Burmeister, 1968; Clymer, 1996; Emans, 1967), but they agree on some. Considering the findings of phonics studies and past teaching experience, we believe the following generalizations are among the most useful:

1. When the letters *c* and *g* are followed by *e, i,* or *y,* they generally have soft sounds: the *s* sound for the letter *c* and the *j* sound for the letter *g.* (Examples: *cent, city, cycle, gem, ginger, gypsy.*) When *c* and *g* are followed by *o, a,* or *u,* they generally have hard sounds: *g* has its own special sound, and *c* has the sound of *k.* (Examples: *cat, cake, cut, go, game, gum.*)

2. When two like consonants are next to each other, only one is sounded. (Examples: *hall, glass.*)

3. *Ch* usually has the sound heard in *church,* although it sometimes sounds like *sh* or *k.* (Examples of usual sound: *child, chill, china.* Examples of *sh* sound: *chef, chevron.* Examples of *k* sound: *chemistry, chord.*)

4. When *kn* are the first two letters in a word, the *k* is not sounded. (Examples: *know, knight.*)

5. When *wr* are the first two letters in a word, the *w* is not sounded. (Examples: *write, wrong.*)

6. When *ck* are the last two letters in a word, the sound of *k* is given. (Examples: *check, brick.*)

7. The sound of a vowel preceding *r* is usually neither long nor short. (Examples: *car, fir, her.*)

8. In the vowel combinations *oa, ee, ai,* and *ay,* the first vowel is generally long and the second one is not sounded. This may also apply to other double vowel combinations. (Examples: *boat, feet, rain, play.*)

9. The double vowels *oi, oy,* and *ou* usually form diphthongs. Whereas the *ow* combination frequently stands for the long *o* sound, it may also form a diphthong. (Examples: *boil, boy, out, now.*)

10. If a word has only one vowel and that vowel is at the end of the word, the vowel usually represents its long sound. (Examples: *me, go.*)

11. If a word has only one vowel and that vowel is *not* at the end of the word, the vowel usually represents its short sound. (Examples: *set, man, cut, hop, list.*)

12. If a word has two vowels and one is a final *e,* the first vowel is usually long and the final *e* is not sounded. (Examples: *cape, cute, cove, kite.*)

Rosso and Emans (1981) tried to determine whether knowledge of phonic generalizations helps children decode unrecognized words and whether children have to be able to state the generalizations to use them. They found statistically significant relationships between knowledge of phonic generalizations and reading achievement, but pointed out that this link does not necessarily indicate a cause-and-effect relationship. They also discovered that "inability to state a phonics rule did not seem to hinder these children's effort to analyze unfamiliar words . . . this study supports Piaget's theory that children in the concrete operations stage of development may encounter difficulty in describing verbally those actions they perform physically" (p. 657). Teachers may need to investigate techniques for teaching phonics generalizations that do not require children to verbalize the generalizations.

It is wise to teach only one generalization at a time, presenting a second only after students have thoroughly learned the first. The existence of exceptions to generalizations should be freely acknowledged, and children should be encouraged to treat the generalizations as *possible* rather than *infallible* clues to pronunciation.

In their summary of *Beginning to Read: Thinking and Learning about Print* by Adams (1990), Stahl, Osborn, and Lehr (1990) emphasize that rote knowledge of abstract generalizations will not produce a skillful decoder. They point out the importance of the connection of generalizations with experience. "Rules are intended to capture the patterns of spelling. But productive use of those patterns depends on relevant experience, not on rote memorization" (p. 83). They conclude that phonics generalizations have only temporary value; in fact, "Once a child has learned to read the spellings to which they pertain, they are superfluous" (p. 126).

Consonants. Although consonant letters are more consistent in the sounds they represent than vowel letters are, they are not perfectly consistent. The following list shows some examples of variations with which a child must contend.

Consonant	Variations	Consonant	Variations
b	board, lamb	n	never, drink
c	cable, city, scene	p	punt, psalm
d	dog, jumped	q(u)	antique, quit
f	fox, of	s	see, sure, his, pleasure, island
g	go, gem, gnat		
h	hit, hour	t	town, listen
j	just, hallelujah	w	work, wrist
k	kitten, knee	x	fox, anxiety, exit
l	lamp, calf	z	zoo, azure, quartz

Consider the cases in which *y* and *w* take on vowel characteristics. Both of these letters represent consonant sounds when they are in the initial position in a word or syllable, but they represent vowel sounds when they are in a final or medial position. For example, *y* represents a consonant sound in the word *yard,* but a vowel sound in the words *dye, myth,* and *baby.* Notice that actually three different vowel sounds are represented by *y* in these words. *W* represents a consonant sound in the word *watch,* but a vowel sound in the word *cow.*

Consonant Digraphs. Several consonant digraphs represent sounds not associated with either of the component parts. These are as follows:

Consonant Digraph	Example	Consonant Digraph	Example
th	then, thick	ph	telephone
ng	sing	gh	rough
sh	shout	ch	chief, chef, chaos

Other consonant digraphs generally represent the usual sound of one of the component parts, as in *wr*ite, *pn*eumonia, and *gn*at. Some sources consider one of the letters in each of these combinations as a "silent" letter and do not refer to these combinations as digraphs.

Vowels. The variability of the sounds represented by vowels has been emphasized before. Some examples of this variability are as follows:

Vowel Letter	Variations
a	ate, cat, want, ball, father, sofa
e	me, red, pretty, kitten, her, sergeant
i	ice, hit, fir, opportunity
o	go, hot, today, women, button, son, work, born
u	use, cut, put, circus, turn

In the examples here, the first variation listed for each vowel is a word in which the long vowel sound, the same as its letter name, is heard. In the second variation the short sound of the vowel is heard. These are generally the first two sounds taught for each vowel.

Another extremely common sound that children need to learn is the schwa sound, a very soft "uh" or grunt usually found in unaccented syllables. It is heard in the following words: sof*a*, kitt*e*n, opportun*i*ty, butt*o*n, circ*u*s. As you can see, each of the vowel letters can represent the schwa sound in some words.

Three types of markings represent the three types of vowel sounds we have discussed:

Marking	Name of Mark	Designation
ā, ē, ī, ō, ū	macron	long vowel sound
ă, ĕ, ĭ, ŏ, ŭ	breve	short vowel sound
ə	schwa	soft "uh" sound

Some dictionaries place no mark at all over a vowel letter that represents the short sound of the vowel.

Vowel Digraphs. Some vowel digraphs represent sounds not associated with either of the letters involved. These are as follows:

Vowel Digraph	Example
au	taught
aw	saw
oo	food, look

Other vowel digraphs generally represent the usual sound of one of the component parts, as in br*ea*k, br*ea*d, b*oa*t, s*ee*d, and *ai*m. Some sources treat one of the letters in these combinations as "silent" and do not refer to them as digraphs.

Diphthongs. There are four common diphthongs, or vowel blends.

Diphthong	Example	Diphthong	Example
oi	foil	ou	bound
oy	toy	ow	cow

Notice that the first two diphthongs listed (*oi* and *oy*) stand for identical sounds, as do the last two (*ou* and *ow*). Remember that the letter combinations *ow* and *ou* are *not always diphthongs*. In the words *snow* and *blow*, *ow* is a vowel digraph representing the long *o* sound. In the word *routine*, *ou* represents the $\overline{oo}$ sound, and in the word *shoulder*, *ou* represents the long *o* sound.

Teaching Strategies

There are two major approaches to phonics instruction: the synthetic and the analytic.

In the *synthetic approach*, the teacher first instructs children in the speech sounds that are associated with individual letters. Because letters and sounds have no inherent relationships, this task is generally accomplished by repeated drill on sound-symbol associations. The teacher may hold up a card on which the letter *b* appears and expect the children to respond with the sound ordinarily associated with that letter. The next step is to blend the sounds together to form words. The teacher encourages the children to pronounce the sounds associated with the letters in rapid succession so that they produce a word or an approximate pronunciation of a word, which they can then recognize and pronounce accurately. This blending process generally begins with two- and three-letter words and proceeds to much longer ones.

Although blending ability is a key factor in the success of a synthetic phonics approach, many commercial materials for reading instruction give little attention to its development. Research indicates that children must master both segmentation of words into their component sounds and blending before they are able to apply phonics skills to the decoding of unknown words and that the ability to segment is a prerequisite for successful blending. Research also indicates that a teacher cannot assume children will automatically transfer the skills they have been taught to unknown words. Direct instruction for transfer is needed to ensure that it will occur (Johnson and Baumann, 1984).

In the synthetic phonics approach, children are sometimes asked to pronounce nonsense syllables because these syllables will appear later in written materials as word parts. Reading words in context does not generally occur until these steps have been repeatedly carried out and the children have developed a moderate stock of words.

The *analytic approach* involves teaching some sight words, followed by teaching the sounds of the letters within those words. Many educators prefer this approach, and it is used in many basal reader series, partly because it avoids the distortion that occurs when consonants are pronounced in isolation. For example, trying to pronounce a *t* in isolation is likely to result in the sounds *tə*. Pronouncing a schwa sound following the consonant can adversely affect the child's blending because the word *tag* must be sounded as *tə-a-gə*. No matter how fast children make those sounds, they are unlikely to come very close to *tag*. With an analytic approach, the teacher would refer to "the sound you hear at the beginning of the word *top,"* when cueing the first sound in *tag.* The same process may be used to introduce other consonants, consonant blends, consonant digraphs, vowels, diphthongs, and vowel digraphs in initial, medial, and final positions. One possible problem when using analytic phonics, however, is that children may not be able to extract an individual sound just from hearing it within a word. Partly for this reason and partly because some analytic phonics instruction is worded in a confusing manner, Adams's (1990) findings seem to indicate that even though trying to isolate phonemes can result in distortion, the advantages of asking students to produce phonemes in isolation can outweigh the disadvantages.

Trachtenburg (1990) suggests a procedure that is basically an analytic approach in which phonics instruction occurs within the context of reading quality children's literature. Here the progression is from the whole literature selection to the phonic element within the selection and back to another whole literature selection for application of the new knowledge. This procedure is consistent with Harp's (1989) statement: "While the process may be broken down to examine individual pieces, before the instruction ends the process should be 'put back together' so that the children see the relationship between the part and the whole" (p. 326).

Trachtenburg's method proceeds as follows:

- First, the teacher reads to the class a literature selection that contains many examples of the phonic element in question. Students may discuss or dramatize the story, when the teacher has finished.

- The teacher introduces the phonic element that is the target for the lesson (long *a, e, i, o,* or *u*; short *a, e, i, o,* or *u*; or some other element) by explaining that the children are going to learn one of the sounds for a specific letter or letter combination.

- Then the teacher writes a portion of the story that contains the target element on the chalkboard or a transparency. The teacher reads this portion of the story aloud, pausing to underline the words containing the target element.

- The teacher identifies the sound involved and asks the children to read the story portion with him or her and listen for the sound. The teacher may suggest a key word that will help them remember the sound in the future.

- The teacher guides practice with the new sound, using a mechanical device in which initial consonants can be varied while the medial vowel remains stationary or a similar device in which both initial and final consonants can be varied. An example of such a device is shown in Activity 3 (page 49) for phonics practice in Part I. The teacher may also provide practice with a similar device that allows sentence parts to be substituted, which enables children to practice the sound in larger language chunks. For example, adjectives, verbs, or adverbs could be varied, as could prepositional phrases, verb phrases, or any other sentence part.

- Finally, the teacher presents another book that has numerous examples of the phonic element. Children may then be allowed to read this book independently, read it in unison from a big book, or read it with a partner, depending on their individual achievement levels.

Trachtenburg (1990) offers the following list of trade books that repeat long and short vowel sounds.

Short a

Flack, Marjorie. *Angus and the Cat.* Doubleday, 1931.

Griffith, Hellen. *Alex and the Cat.* Greenwillow, 1982.

Kent, Jack. *The Fat Cat.* Scholastic, 1971.

Most, Bernard. *There's an Ant in Anthony.* William Morrow, 1980.

Nodset, Joan. *Who Took the Farmer's Hat?* Harper & Row, 1963.

Robins, Joan. *Addie Meets Max.* Harper & Row, 1985.

Schmidt, Karen. *The Gingerbread Man.* Scholastic, 1985.

Seuss, Dr. *The Cat in the Hat.* Random House, 1957.

Long a

Aardema, Verna. *Bringing the Rain to Kapiti Plain.* Dial, 1981.

Bang, Molly. *The Paper Crane.* Greenwillow, 1985.

Blume, Judy. *The Pain and the Great One.* Bradbury, 1974.

Byars, Betsy. *The Lace Snail.* Viking, 1975.

Henkes, Kevin. *Sheila Rae, the Brave.* Greenwillow, 1987.

Hines, Anna G. *Taste the Raindrops.* Greenwillow, 1983.

Short and long a

Aliki. *Jack and Jake.* Greenwillow, 1986.

Slobodkina, Esphyr. *Caps for Sale.* Addison-Wesley, 1940.

Short e

Ets, Marie Hall. *Elephant in a Well.* Viking, 1972.

Galdone, Paul. *The Little Red Hen.* Scholastic, 1973.

Ness, Evaline. *Yeck Eck.* E. P. Dutton, 1974.

Shecter, Ben. *Hester the Jester.* Harper & Row, 1977.

Thayer, Jane. *I Don't Believe in Elves.* William Morrow, 1975.

Wing, Henry Ritchet. *Ten Pennies for Candy.* Holt, Rinehart & Winston, 1963.

Long e

Galdone, Paul. *Little Bo-Peep.* Clarion/Ticknor & Fields, 1986.

Keller, Holly. *Ten Sleepy Sheep.* Greenwillow, 1983.

Martin, Bill. *Brown Bear, Brown Bear, What Do You See?* Henry Holt, 1967.

Oppenheim, Joanne. *Have You Seen Trees?* Young Scott Books, 1967.

Soule, Jean C. *Never Tease a Weasel.* Parents' Magazine Press, 1964.

Thomas, Patricia. *"Stand Back," Said the Elephant, "I'm Going to Sneeze!"* Lothrop, Lee & Shepard, 1971.

Short i

Browne, Anthony. *Willy the Wimp*. Alfred A. Knopf, 1984.

Ets, Marie Hall. *Gilberto and the Wind*. Viking, 1966.

Hutchins, Pat. *Titch*. Macmillan, 1971.

Keats, Ezra Jack. *Whistle for Willie*. Viking, 1964.

Lewis, Thomas P. *Call for Mr. Sniff*. Harper & Row, 1981.

Lobel, Arnold. *Small Pig*. Harper & Row, 1969.

McPhail, David. *Fix-It*. E. P. Dutton, 1984.

Patrick, Gloria. *This Is . . .* Carolrhoda, 1970.

Robins, Joan. *My Brother, Will*. Greenwillow, 1986.

Long i

Berenstain, Stan and Jan. *The Bike Lesson*. Random House, 1964.

Cameron, John. *If Mice Could Fly*. Atheneum, 1979.

Cole, Sheila. *When the Tide Is Low*. Lothrop, Lee & Shepard, 1985.

Gelman, Rita. *Why Can't I Fly?* Scholastic, 1976.

Hazen, Barbara S. *Tight Times*. Viking, 1979.

Short o

Benchley, Nathaniel. *Oscar Otter*. Harper & Row, 1966.

Dunrea, Olivier. *Mogwogs on the March!* Holiday House, 1985.

Emberley, Barbara. *Drummer Hoff*. Prentice-Hall, 1967.

McKissack, Patricia C. *Flossie & the Fox*. Dial, 1986.

Miller, Patricia, and Iran Seligman. *Big Frogs, Little Frogs*. Holt, Rinehart & Winston, 1963.

Rice, Eve. "The Frog and the Ox" from *Once in a Wood*. Greenwillow, 1979.

Seuss, Dr. *Fox in Socks*. Random House, 1965.

Long o

Cole, Brock. *The Giant's Toe*. Farrar, Straus & Giroux, 1986.

Gerstein, Mordicai. *Roll Over!* Crown, 1984.

Johnston, Tony. *The Adventures of Mole and Troll*. G. P. Putnam's Sons, 1972.

Johnston, Tony. *Night Noises and Other Mole and Troll Stories*. G. P. Putnam's Sons, 1977.

Shulevitz, Uri. *One Monday Morning*. Charles Scribner's Sons, 1967.

Tresselt, Alvin. *White Snow, Bright Snow*. Lothrop, Lee & Shepard, 1947.

Short u

Carroll, Ruth. *Where's the Bunny?* Henry Z. Walck, 1950.

Cooney, Nancy E. *Donald Says Thumbs Down*. G. P. Putnam's Sons, 1987.

Friskey, Margaret. *Seven Little Ducks*. Children's Press, 1940.

Lorenz, Lee. *Big Gus and Little Gus*. Prentice-Hall, 1982.

Marshall, James. *The Cut-Ups*. Viking Kestrel, 1984.

Udry, Janice May. *Thump and Plunk*. Harper & Row, 1981.

Yashima, Taro. *Umbrella*. Viking Penguin, 1958.

Long u

Lobel, Anita. *The Troll Music*. Harper & Row, 1966.

Segal, Lore. *Tell Me a Trudy*. Farrar, Straus & Giroux, 1977.

Slobodkin, Louis. *"Excuse Me—Certainly!"* Vanguard Press, 1959.

The following Focus on Strategies tells how a teacher introduced the long *e* sound in story context, thus using an analytic approach to phonics.

**Focus on
Strategies**

Teaching Phonics Through Literature

Ms. Mahan started her class by reading the predictable book *Peanut Butter and Jelly* (JoAnne Nelson, Modern Curriculum Press, 1989) to her first graders. By the time she got to page 13, the children were chiming in on the repeated line "But peanut butter and jelly is my favorite thing to eat," as she always encouraged the children to do when they discovered the predictable pattern. When the story had been completed, the teacher responded to requests to "read it again" by doing so. This time the children joined in on the repeated line from the beginning.

The children discussed the story, and Ms. Mahan made a list on the board of the children's personal favorite things to eat.

Then Ms. Mahan wrote the letter combination *ea* on the board. One of the words on the list of the children's favorite foods was *beans.* Another one was *peanuts.* She pronounced each of these words and pointed out that both contained a long *e* sound. Then she displayed transparencies of pages from the story *Peanut Butter and Jelly.* As she read page 5, she underlined the words *meat, peanut,* and *eat.* She then reread each underlined word and asked the children to listen to the sounds. She told the class that the letter combination *ea* often has the long *e* sound. Then she read the words again as they listened specifically for the long *e* sound.

She proceeded to display subsequent pages from the story, asking the children to watch for the *ea* combination in the words and raise their hands when they saw it. When hands were raised, she let the children identify the words with the *ea* combination. Then the children listened for the long *e* sound in each word. The following words from this story fit this pattern: *eat, meat, peanut, cream, wheat, treat, heat,* and *beat.* They also found the word *cereal* and recognized that they heard the long *e* sound. Since they had not yet had instruction on syllabication or schwa sounds, Ms. Mahan simply agreed that there was a long *e* sound after the *r* and went on to the next word. On page 18 they saw a word with the *ea* combination that did not have the long *e* sound: *bread.* The presence of this word allowed Ms. Mahan to point out that sounds are not always consistent and that the sound-letter clues only helped the children make "best guesses" about pronunciations, not absolute certainties.

Ms. Mahan then encouraged the children to play with the words that had been located. She wrote *eat* on the board and asked them how to turn it into *meat.* She let Tammy come to the board and add the needed letter. Then she wrote *eat* again and asked who could turn it into *wheat,* then *treat,* then *heat,* then *beat.* Finally, she branched out from words that were found directly in the story and let the children form *neat* and *seat.* She also let them transform *cream* into *team, seam,* and *dream* by removing the initial blend and replacing it with other letters.

(continued)

> Then Ms. Mahan pointed out that sometimes there are several ways to spell a particular sound. She used the transparencies of the story again, encouraging the children to listen for the long *e* sound in words other than the ones already underlined. They located *sweet, street, beet, even,* and *cheese.* Ms. Mahan asked if they could suggest any other letter patterns that could spell the long *e* sound. They quickly identified the *ee* combination, and eventually Tommy said that the *e* by itself could also spell the sound.
>
> Ms. Mahan then shared the books *Ten Sleepy Sheep* (Holly Keller, Greenwillow, 1983) and *Never Tease a Weasel* (Jean C. Soule, Parents' Magazine Press, 1964) with the children and put them in the reading center, along with *Peanut Butter and Jelly,* to be reread by the children independently or with partners.
>
> The children were then given time to write their own stories about favorite foods. Ms. Mahan asked them to notice which words had the long *e* sound as they wrote. She let them share their stories orally with small groups of their peers.

The following two sample lesson plans further illustrate the analytic method. The first one is *inductive*: the children look at a number of specific examples related to a generalization and then derive the generalization. The second is *deductive*: the teacher states a generalization and then has the children apply the generalization in decoding unfamiliar words.

Model Activities

Analytic-Inductive Lesson Plan for Initial Consonant

Write on the chalkboard the following words, all of which the children have learned previously as sight words:

dog	did
daddy	donkey
do	Dan

Ask the children to listen carefully as you pronounce the words. Then ask: "Did any parts of these words sound the same?" If you receive an affirmative reply, ask: "What part sounded the same?" This should elicit the answer that the first sound in each word is the same or that the words sound alike at the beginning.

Next, ask the children to look carefully at the words written on the board. Ask: "Do you see anything that is the same in all these words?" This should elicit the answer that all of the words have the same first letter or all of the words start with *d.*

Then ask what the children can conclude about words that begin with the letter *d.* The expected answer is that words that begin with the letter *d* sound the same at the beginning as the word *dog* (or any other word on their list).

Next, invite the children to name other words that have the same beginning sound as *dog.* Write each word on the board. Ask the children to observe the words and draw another conclusion. They may say, "Words that sound the same at the beginning as the word *dog* begin with the letter *d.*"

Ask the children to watch for words in their reading that begin with the letter *d* to check the accuracy of their conclusions.

Model Activities

Analytic-Deductive Lesson Plan for Soft Sound of *c*

Tell the children: "When the letter *c* is followed by *e, i,* or *y,* it generally has its soft sound, which is the sound you have learned for the letter *s*." Write the following examples on the chalkboard: *city, cycle,* and *cent.* Point out that in *cycle* only the *c* that is followed by *y* has the soft sound. Follow this presentation with an activity designed to check the children's understanding of the generalization. The activity might involve a worksheet with items like this:

Directions: Place a check beside the words that contain a soft *c* sound.

_____ cite   _____ cider

_____ cape   _____ cord

_____ cede   _____ cymbal

_____ cut   _____ cod

_____ cell

The soft *c* sound is the sound we have learned for the letter _____ .

An approach that has some aspects of both the synthetic and analytic approaches is the teaching of *onsets* and *rimes*. In this approach, the teacher breaks down a syllable into the part of the syllable before the vowel (onset) and the remainder of the syllable (rime) that begins with the vowel. In the past, these rimes were referred to as *phonograms*. (See Example 1.)

Example 1	*Onsets and Rimes*	
Word	*Onset*	*Rime*
black	bl–	–ack
may	m–	–ay
am	—	am

In one rime-based instructional program, the Benchmark Word Identification Program, children compare an unknown word to familiar words in order to decode the words by analogy. Then they use context to check their predictions (Stahl, 1992; Gaskins et al., 1988; Gaskins et al., 1991; Gaskins et al., 1997). Such an approach is called an *analogy approach* or a *compare/contrast approach*. The children are taught an initial set of "key words," containing the phonograms or rimes. After comparing the unknown word to a known one and coming up with a tentative decision about the pronunciation of the unknown word, a child would be expected to check to see whether the new word produced made sense in the sentence in which it was found. According to Adams (1990), the letter-sound correspondences in rimes are more stable than the correspondences found when the letters are taken in isolation.

Gunning (1995) proposes a system for phonics instruction called Word Building that uses onsets and rimes. The class first builds words by adding onsets to rimes, then by adding rimes to onsets. This is followed by reading that allows practice with the patterns under consideration. Gunning also suggests having the students make words with magnetic letters, mix the letters up and reassemble the words, and then observe how each word changes as letters are added and removed, a process advocated by Clay (1993). Students are shown how to decode hard words by using phonic elements that they have learned. This approach can be used with multisyllabic words as well as with single-syllable words.

Gaskins and others (1991) found that direct instruction was useful in teaching phonics through the analogy approach. In every lesson, teachers inform the children about *"what* they are going to teach, *why* it is important, *when* it can be used, and *how* to use it" (p. 215). This explanation is followed by teacher modeling and group and individual guided practice for the students. Every-pupil response activities and teacher feedback are important program features. Key words are introduced through a structured language experience activity (the writing of a group story with the key words just presented). Phonemic awareness activities are also included to facilitate the learning of onsets such as the initial consonant *f* or the initial consonant blend *fr*. Gaskins and others (1996/1997; 1997) stress the need for students to be reflective and analytic about words and spelling patterns. They also emphasize that the students must learn the importance of analyzing all letters in a word and relating the letters to sounds so that they can retrieve the word later. Students do this by matching sounds to letters as they "stretch out" the pronunciation of the words. Self-talk about the procedure is encouraged. The following Model Activity shows use of an analogy or compare/contrast approach.

Model Activities

Analogy or Compare/Contrast Approach

The teacher writes the key words *be* and *rain* on the board and pronounces them. Then he or she writes: "The student hopes to <u>remain</u> in that group." The teacher verbalizes the thought pattern needed to decode the word in this way: "If this (pointing to *be*) is *be,* then this is probably *re.* If this (pointing to *rain*) is *rain,* then this is probably *main."* (Note: The sounds of the initial consonants *r* and *m* must have been taught previously.) The teacher continues: "The word is *remain.* Does that make sense in the context?" After receiving an affir-

mative reply, the teacher says: "Yes, *remain* means to stay."

Then the teacher provides a list of key words the students have already studied and turned into sight words, as well as several paragraphs, preferably from a story they are about to read, with difficult words underlined. The teacher asks the students to decode these underlined words, using the key words and the strategy that has just been modeled. After the children have worked at this task independently, the teacher calls on several students to verbalize their strategies for the difficult words.

Spiegel (1990) recommends the commercial games *Road Race* (Carpenter, Curriculum Associates, 1987) and *Word Trek* (Collgrove, DLM, 1977) as educationally valid decoding games that work well with the compare/contrast, onset-rime, and word family approaches to phonics instruction.

Ehri and Robbins (1992) found that students needed some knowledge of phoneme-grapheme correspondences in order to be able to use onset-rime units. Bruck and Treiman (1992) discovered that beginning readers can use analogies, but tend to rely more on individual phoneme-grapheme correspondences to decode new words. Their findings suggest that students need instruction on individual phoneme-grapheme correspondences, especially for vowels, rather than just on relationships between groups of phonemes and groups of graphemes. They warn that rime instruction is not sufficient by itself.

Johnson and Baumann (1984) cite research indicating that "programs emphasizing a phonics or code approach to word identification produce superior word-calling ability when compared to programs applying an analytic phonics or meaning emphasis" (p. 590). But, they continue, "there seem to be distinct differences in the quality of error responses made by children instructed in the two general methodologies—readers' errors tend to be real words, meaningful, and syntactically appropriate when instruction emphasizes meaning, whereas code-emphasis word-identification instruction results in more nonword errors that are graphically and aurally like the mispronounced words" (p. 590). Because the goal of reading is comprehension, not word calling, the analytic approach, which uses meaning-emphasis techniques, seems to be the better choice for instruction.

Teachers should keep in mind a caution about the teaching of phonics generalizations that involve the use of such terms as *sound* and *word*. Studies by Reid and Downing indicate that young children (five year olds) have trouble understanding terms used to talk about language, such as *word, letter,* and *sound* (Downing, 1973), and Meltzer and Herse (1969) found that first-grade children do not always know where printed words begin and end. In addition, Tovey (1980) found that the group of second through sixth graders he studied had difficulty in dealing with abstract phonics terms such as *consonant, consonant blend, consonant digraph, vowel digraph, diphthong, possessive, inflectional ending,* and others. His study also showed that the children had learned sound-symbol associations without being able to define the phonics terms involved. Before teaching a lesson using linguistic terms, the teacher should check to be sure that students grasp such concepts. Technical terminology should be deemphasized when working with students who have not mastered the terms.

Cordts (1965) suggests using key words to help children learn the sounds associated with vowels, consonants, vowel digraphs, consonant digraphs, diphthongs, and consonant blends. In all cases, these words should already be part of the children's sight vocabularies. Cordts suggests that a key word for a vowel sound be one that contains that vowel sound and can be pictured, whereas a key word for a consonant sound should be one that can be pictured and has that consonant sound at the end. She believes that consonant sounds can be heard more clearly at the ends than at the beginnings of words.

Other authorities also encourage the use of key words, but most suggest using words with the consonant sounds at the beginning. The sounds may be harder to distinguish, but usable key words are much easier to find when initial sounds are used.

Key words are valuable in helping children remember sound-symbol associations that are not inherently meaningful. People remember new things through associations with things they already know. The more associations a person has for an abstract relationship, such as the letter *d* and the sound of *d*, the more quickly that person will learn to link the sound and the symbol. The person's retention of this connection will also be more accurate. Schell (1978) refers to a third-grade boy who chose as key words for the consonant blends *dr, fr,* and *sp* the character names *Dracula, Frankenstein,* and *Spiderman.* These associations were both concrete and personal for him. The characters were drawn on key-word cards to aid his memory of the associations.

Consonant substitution activities are useful for helping students see how their knowledge of some words helps them to decode other words. Following is a Model Activity for teaching consonant substitution.

Model Activities

Consonant Substitution

Write a known word, such as *pat,* on the board and ask the students to pronounce the word. Then write on the board a letter for which the sound has been taught (for example, *m*). If the letter sound can be pronounced in isolation without distortion, ask the students to do so; if not, ask for a word beginning with this sound. Then ask the students to leave the *p* sound off when they pronounce the word on the board. They will respond with *at.* Next, ask them to put the *m* sound in front of the *at,* and they will produce *mat.* The same process is followed with other sounds, such as *s, r,* and *b.*

This procedure is also useful with sounds at the ends of words or in medial positions. Vowel substitution activities, in which you may start with a known word and have the students omit the vowel sound and substitute a different one (for example: s*a*t, s*e*t, s*i*t; p*a*t, p*e*t, p*i*t, p*o*t), can also be helpful.

Cunningham and Cunningham (1992) suggest an activity called Making Words, which is a guided group invented-spelling instructional strategy designed to take advantage of the values of writing with invented spelling while offering a more direct instructional procedure. In it the children use the letters of a long word to spell short words of varying lengths, eventually trying to actually spell the long word from which the others were made. They then sort the words they have made according to a variety of patterns. This activity is designed to be used along with writing activities that involve invented spelling.

Oleneski (1992) used the jump rope rhyme "Teddy Bear" to teach sounds in an analytic manner with authentic material. She duplicated the rhyme, which the children knew well, and let them engage in activities such as reading it and sequencing its parts with sentence strips. Then she covered up certain words and had the children figure out what these words were. She then asked them to predict which letters would represent the beginning and ending sounds of the target words. Students continued to use the poem for reading and writing activities to keep the instruction on sounds in context. This procedure could be used with other jump-rope rhymes or ball-bouncing rhymes.

Drill on letter-sound associations need not be dull. Teachers can use many game activities, and activities that are more formal will not become boring if they are not overused. When planning games, teachers should always remember that, although competitive situations are motivational for some youngsters, other children are adversely affected by being placed in win/lose situations, especially if they have little hope of being winners at least part of the time. Game situations in which children cooperate or in which they compete with *their own previous records* rather than with one another are often more acceptable. Following are some practical examples of both competitive and noncompetitive games.

Activities

1. Give each child a sheet of paper that is blank except for a letter at the top. Have the children draw pictures of as many items as they can think of that have names beginning with the sound of the letter at the top of the page. Declare the child with the most correct responses the winner.

2. Make five decorated boxes, and label each box with a short vowel. Have the children locate pictures of objects whose names contain the short vowel sounds and file them in the appropriate boxes. Each day take out the pictures, ask the children to pronounce the names, and check to see if the appropriate sounds are present. Do the same thing with long vowel sounds, consonant sounds, consonant blends, digraphs, diphthongs, and rhyming words.

3. Place a familiar word ending on a cardboard disk like the one pictured here. Pull a strip of cardboard with initial consonants on it through an opening cut in the disk. Show the children how to pull the strip through the disk, pronouncing each word that is formed.

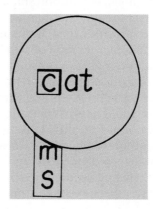

4. Divide the children into two groups. Give half of them initial consonant, consonant blend, or consonant digraph cards. Give the other half word-ending cards. Instruct the children to pair up with other children holding word parts that combine with their parts to form real words. Have each pair hold up their cards and pronounce the word they have made when they have located a combination. Then let them search for other possible combinations for their word parts.

5. Use riddles. For example: "I have in mind a word that rhymes with *far*. We ride in it. It's called a _____ ."

6. Let the children find a hidden picture by shading in all the spaces that contain words with long vowel sounds.

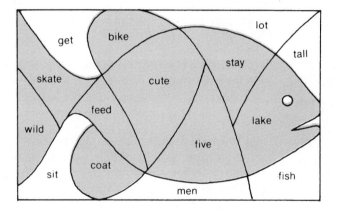

To be effective, practice exercises should always be preceded by instruction and followed by feedback on results. The absence of prior instruction may cause students to practice the wrong response. Feedback, which should come either directly from the teacher or through a self-correcting procedure (posted answers, for example), will inform students of errors immediately so that they do not learn incorrect responses. When students fail to see reasons for errors, the teacher will need to provide explanations and reteach the strategy or skill.

A phonics strategy or skill is a means to an end, not an end in itself. Readers who can recognize words without resorting to letter-by-letter sounding will recognize them more quickly than those who must sound out the words, and the process will interfere less with their train of thought than sounding out the words would have. When the words to be recognized are seen in context, as in most normal reading activities, the sound of the first letter alone may elicit recognition of the whole word. Context clues can provide a child with an idea about the word's identity, and the initial sound can be used to verify an educated guess. This procedure is efficient and is a good way to identify unfamiliar words quickly. Of course, the ultimate goal of instruction in phonics and other word identification skills is to turn initially unfamiliar words into automatically recognized sight words.

Structural Analysis

Structural analysis is closely related to phonics and has several significant facets:

1. Inflectional endings
2. Prefixes and suffixes
3. Contractions
4. Compound words
5. Syllabication and accents

Structural analysis strategies and skills enable children to decode unfamiliar words by using units larger than single graphemes; this procedure generally expedites the decoding process. Structural analysis can also help in understanding word meanings, a function discussed in Part II.

Inflectional Endings

Inflectional endings are added to nouns to change number, case, or gender; added to verbs to change tense or person; and added to adjectives to change degree. They may also change a word's part of speech. Since inflectional endings are letters or groups of letters added to the endings of root words, some people call them *inflectional suffixes*. Here are some examples of words with inflectional endings.

Root Word	New Word	Change
boy	boys	Singular noun changed to plural noun
host	hostess	Gender of noun changed from masculine to feminine
Karen	Karen's	Proper noun altered to show possession (change of case)
look	looked	Verb changed from present tense to past tense
make	makes	Verb changed from first or second person singular to third person singular
mean	meaner	Simple form of adjective changed to the comparative form
happy	happily	Adjective changed to adverb

Generally, the first inflectional ending to which children are exposed is *-s*. This ending often appears in early reading materials and should be learned early in the first grade. Other inflectional endings children are likely to encounter in these early materials are *-ing* and *-ed.*

A child can be shown the effect of the addition of an *-s* to a singular noun through use of illustrations of single and multiple objects. An activity such as that shown in the following Model Activity: Recognizing Inflectional Ending -*s* can be used to practice this skill. A second Model Activity for various inflectional endings demonstrates further possibilities for practice with different inflectional endings.

Recognizing Inflectional Ending -*s*

Model Activities

Give the following practice sheet to the children.

Ask the children to read and follow the directions. Then go over the practice sheet with them orally, asking how each word that shows more than one thing looks different from the word that shows only one thing. They should come to the conclusion that -*s* at the ends of the words indicates more than one thing.

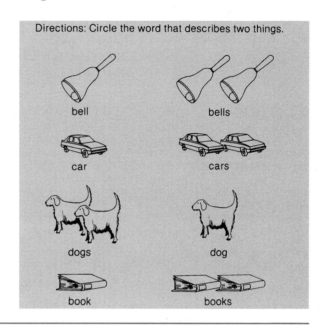

Directions: Circle the word that describes two things.

bell   bells

car   cars

dogs   dog

book   books

Recognizing Inflectional Endings

Model Activities

Write on the board sentences containing inflectional endings that have already been discussed, taken from a book that has been shared in class. Ask the children to read the sentences silently, looking for the inflectional endings they have studied in class. After the silent reading, let volunteers go to the board, circle the inflectional endings in the sentences, and tell how each ending affects word meaning or word use.

You may not wish to use all possible examples from the book in this activity. Instead, you can encourage students to go back to the book itself, either individually or in pairs, locate the inflectional endings under consideration, and make a list of the words they find. These words can be discussed later in a group discussion, with the students finding the words in the story and reading the sentences in which they appear.

As an example, *Ox-Cart Man* (Hall, Puffin Books, 1979) could be used for sentences containing the words *backed, filled, packed, sheared, spinning, pairs, mittens, candles, shingles, brooms, carved, borrowed, potatoes, counted, apples, honeycombs, turnips, cabbages, maples, tapped, boiled, feathers, collected, waved, walked, ox's, days, hills, valleys, streams, farms, villages, kissed, pockets, coins, pounds, candies, tucked, kettle's, waiting, stitching, whittling, cooked, sawed, embroidered, trees, knitted, planted, blossoms, bloomed, bees, starting, squawked, dropping,* and *clouds.* From this short book, you could effectively re-

view the inflectional endings *-ed, -s, -'s,* and *-ing.* You may decide to handle each inflectional ending in a separate lesson.

Children in the primary grades are frequently exposed to the possessive case formed by *-'s.* Here is an activity designed for work with this inflectional ending.

Model Activities

Using *-'s* for the Singular Possessive

Tell the children: "When I say, 'This is the book of my brother,' I mean that the book belongs to my brother. Another, shorter, way to say the same thing is 'This is my brother's book.' The *apostrophe s* on the end of the word *brother* shows that the noun following *brother* (*book*) belongs to *brother.*"

Have the children examine stories they have read recently for examples of the use of *-'s.* Let them read the sentences they found that contained *-'s* and tell the meanings of the phrases in which it occurs.

Prefixes and Suffixes

Prefixes and suffixes are *affixes,* letters or sequences of letters that are added to root words to change their meanings and/or parts of speech. A *prefix* is placed before a root word, and a *suffix* is placed after a root word.

Children can learn the pronunciations and meanings of some common prefixes and suffixes. Good readers learn to recognize common prefixes and suffixes instantly; this helps them recognize words more rapidly than they could if they had to resort to sounding each word letter by letter. Knowledge of prefixes and suffixes can help readers decipher the meanings as well as the pronunciations of unfamiliar words.

The suffixes *-ment, -ous, -tion,* and *-sion* have especially consistent pronunciations and thus are particularly useful to know. The suffixes *-ment* and *-ous* generally have the pronunciations heard in the words *treatment* and *joyous.* The suffixes *-tion* and *-sion* have the sound of *shun,* as heard in the words *education* and *mission.*

Whereas prefixes simply modify the meanings of the root words, suffixes may change the parts of speech as well as modify the meanings. Some of the resulting modifications are listed here.

Root Word	Affix	New Word	New Meaning or Change
happy	un-	unhappy	not happy
amuse	-ment	amusement	verb is changed to noun
worth	-less	worthless	meaning is opposite of original meaning

Use activities like the two following Model Activities.

Recognition of Prefixes and Suffixes

After instruction in prefixes and suffixes, give the students duplicated sheets containing paragraphs from a story that has just been shared in class. Ask them to circle the prefixes and suffixes they see in the paragraphs, working independently. Then divide them into small groups and have them compare and discuss their responses. Each group should come to an agreement about the correct answers. Finally, check the group responses in a whole-class discussion, calling on small-group representatives to give each group's responses to various items.

For example, in *Nadia the Willful* (Alexander, Knopf, 1983), the following words appear: *stubbornness, willful, kindness, graciousness, return, emptiness, punishment, remind, uneasily, hardness, coldness, unhappiness, bitterness, inside, recall, recalled, unbidden, happiness, sharpness,* and *forward.* Some of the words occur several times. The paragraphs in which these words appear can be duplicated for this exercise.

Not all of the words need to be used in a single lesson. You may wish to use one prefix or suffix at a time.

Adding Prefixes and Suffixes

Write the following root words on the chalkboard.

1. agree   2. move   3. construct

Ask the children to write on their papers as many new words as they can by adding prefixes and suffixes to these root words. Then have the children form small groups and share the words they have formed with the other group members. Group members may question some of the words their classmates have

formed and may consult reference books or the teacher to confirm or discredit words formed. Then representatives from the small groups may share the groups' word collections with the rest of the class.

The children may then be encouraged to produce small-group or individual stories using some of the words they constructed. These stories can be shared orally or in written form (perhaps on the bulletin board or in a reading center) with the rest of the class.

In the third and fourth grades, children begin to encounter more words that contain prefixes, suffixes, or both (White, Sowell, and Yanagihara, 1989; Nagy and Anderson, 1984). White, Sowell, and Yanagihara (1989) have identified nine prefixes (*un-; re-; in-, im-, ir-* [meaning *not*]; *dis-; en-, em-; non-; in-, im-* [meaning *in* or *into*]; *over-* [meaning *too much*]; and *mis-*) that cover 76 percent of the prefixed words in the *Word Frequency Book* (Carroll, Davies, and Richman, 1971). They recommend that these prefixes be taught systematically during grades three through five, beginning with *un-,* which alone accounts for 26 percent of the prefixed words. An analysis of their word counts would lead us to add *sub-, pre-, inter-,* and *fore-* to the recommended list, since they occur as frequently as *over-* and *mis-,* thereby covering 88 percent of the prefixed words.

White, Sowell, and Yanagihara (1989) have identified ten suffixes and inflectional endings that are part of 85 percent of the suffixed words in the *Word Frequency Book: -s, -es; -ed; -ing; -ly; -er, -or* (agentive); *-ion, -tion, -ation, -ition; -ible, -able; -al, -ial; -y;* and *-ness.* The three inflectional endings *-s/-es, -ed,* and *-ing* alone account for 65 percent of the incidences of suffixed words in the sample.

Contractions

The apostrophe used in contractions indicates that one or more letters have been left out when two words were combined into one word. Children need to be able to recognize the original words from which the contractions were formed. The following are common contractions, with their meanings, that teachers should present to children:

can't/cannot	I'd/I had or I would	I'll/I will	shouldn't/ should not
couldn't/could not		I'm/I am	
	they'd/they had or they would	I've/I have	we've/we have
didn't/did not		isn't/is not	won't/will not
don't/do not	they'll/they will	let's/let us	wouldn't/would not
hadn't/had not	they're/they are		
hasn't/has not	they've/they have	she'd/she would or she had	you'll/you will
he'll/he will	wasn't/was not	she'll/she will	you're/you are
he's/he is or he has	we're/we are	she's/she is or she has	you've/you have
	weren't/were not		

The teacher may wish to teach contractions in related groups—for example, those in which *not* is the reduced part, those in which *have* is the reduced part, and so on. Students should locate these contractions and their uncontracted referents in context and use them in writing to enhance their learning.

Compound Words

Compound words consist of two (or occasionally three) words that have been joined together to form a new word. The original pronunciations of the component words are usually maintained, and their meanings are connected to form the meaning of the new word: *dishpan,* for example, is a pan in which dishes are washed. Children can be asked to underline or circle component parts of compound words or to put together familiar compound words as practice activities. An exercise for compound words follows.

Model Activities

Recognizing Parts of Compound Words

Display a page from a big book (or a transparency made from a regular-size book) that contains several compound words. Let students come to the book (or the projected image) and point out the words that are made up of two or more words (for example, in *Song and Dance Man* [Acker-man, Knopf, 1988], the words *Grandpa, Grandma, cardboard, leather-trimmed, inside, half-moon, spotlight, woodpecker, somebody's, bathroom, gold-tipped,* and *stairway*). Write the words on the chalkboard. Let volunteers come to the board and circle the separate words that make up each compound word. Have a class discussion about the way to decide how to pronounce compound words.

Syllabication/Accent

Since many phonics generalizations apply not only to one-syllable words but also to syllables within longer words, many people believe that breaking words into syllables can help determine pronunciation. Some research indicates, however, that syllabication is usually done after the reader has recognized the word and that readers use the sounds to determine syllabication rather than syllabication to determine the sounds (Glass, 1967). If this procedure is the one children normally use in attacking words, syllabication would seem to be of little use in a word analysis program. On the other hand, many authorities firmly believe that syllabication is helpful in decoding words. For this reason, a textbook on reading methods would be incomplete without discussions of syllabication and a related topic, stress or accent.

A *syllable* is a letter or group of letters that forms a pronunciation unit. Every syllable contains a vowel sound. In fact, a vowel sound may form a syllable by itself (*a/mong*). Only in a syllable that contains a diphthong is there more than one vowel sound. Diphthongs are treated as single units, although they are actually vowel blends. While each syllable has only one vowel sound or diphthong, a syllable may have more than one vowel letter. Letters and sounds should not be confused. The word *peeve,* for example, has three vowel letters, but the only vowel sound is the long *e* sound. Therefore, *peeve* contains only one syllable.

There are two types of syllables: open and closed. Open syllables end in vowel sounds; closed syllables end in consonant sounds. Syllables may in turn be classified as accented (given greater stress) or unaccented (given little stress). Accent has much to do with the vowel sound we hear in a syllable. Multisyllabic words may have primary (strongest), secondary (second strongest), and even tertiary (third strongest) accents. The vowel sound of an open accented syllable is usually long (*mī' nus, bā' sin*); the second syllable of each of these example words is unaccented, and the vowel sound represented is the schwa, often found in unaccented syllables. A single vowel in a closed accented syllable generally has its short sound, unless it is influenced by another sound in that syllable (*căp' sule, cär' go*).

Following are several useful generalizations concerning syllabication and accent:

1. Words contain as many syllables as they have vowel sounds (counting diphthongs as a unit). Examples: *se/vere* (final *e* has no sound); *break* (*e* is not sounded); *so/lo* (both vowels are sounded); *oil* (diphthong is treated as a unit).

2. In a word with more than one sounded vowel, when the first vowel is followed by two consonants, the division is generally between the two consonants. Examples: *mar/ry, tim/ber.* If the two consonants are identical, the second one is not sounded.

3. Consonant blends and consonant digraphs are treated as units and are not divided. Examples: *ma/chine, a/bridge.*

4. In a word with more than one sounded vowel, when the first vowel is followed by only one consonant or consonant digraph, the division is generally after the vowel. Examples: *ma/jor, ri/val* (long initial vowel sounds). There are, however, many exceptions to this rule, which make it less useful. Examples: *rob/in, hab/it* (short initial vowel sounds).

5. When a word ends in *-le* preceded by a consonant, the preceding consonant plus *-le* constitute the final syllable of the word. This syllable is never accented, and the vowel sound heard in it is the schwa. Examples: *can/dle, ta/ble.*

6. Prefixes and suffixes generally form separate syllables. Examples: *dis/taste/ful, pre/dic/tion.*

7. A compound word is divided between the two words that form the compound, as well as between syllables within the component words. Examples: *snow/man, thun/der/storm.*

8. Prefixes and suffixes are usually not accented. Example: *dis/grace' ful.*

9. Words that can be used as both verbs and nouns are accented on the second syllable when used as verbs and on the first syllable when used as nouns. Examples: *pre/sent'* —verb; *pres' ent*—noun.

10. In two-syllable root words, the first syllable is usually accented, unless the second syllable has two vowel letters. Examples: *rock' et, pa/rade'.*

11. Words containing three or more syllables are likely to have secondary (and perhaps tertiary) accents, in addition to primary accents. Example: *reg' i/men/ta' tion.*

Readiness for learning syllabication includes the ability to hear syllables as pronunciation units. Here is an early exercise on syllabication.

**Model
Activities**

Syllabication

Teachers can have children as young as first graders listen to words and clap for every syllable heard. Ask the children to say words aloud and listen for the syllables. Let them clap once for each syllable as it is pronounced. Include both single-syllable and multisyllabic words in the exercise.

Some example words you may use are as follows:

1. rule	5. disagreement
2. table	6. person
3. meaningful	7. fingertip
4. middle	8. name

Generalizations about syllabication can be taught using the same process as that for phonic generalizations, described earlier in this *Primer*. The teacher can present many examples of a particular generalization and lead the children to state the generalization.

Waugh and Howell (1975) point out that in dictionaries it is the syllable divisions in the phonetic respellings, rather than the ones indicated in the boldface entry words, that are useful to students in pronouncing unfamiliar words. The divisions of the boldface entry words are a guide for hyphenations in writing, not for word pronunciation.

Accentuation generally is not taught until children have a good background in word attack skills and is often presented in conjunction with dictionary study as a tool for word attack. More will be said on this topic in the next section of this primer.

Dictionary Study

Dictionaries are valuable tools that can help in completing many kinds of reading tasks. They can help students determine pronunciations, meanings, derivations, and parts of speech for words they encounter in reading activities. They can also help with word spellings, if children have some idea of how the words are spelled and need only to confirm the order of letters within the words. Picture dictionaries are used primarily for sight word recognition and spelling assistance. Children can be introduced to picture dictionaries as early as the first grade. They can learn how dictionaries are put together and how they function by making their own picture dictionaries. Intermediate-grade pupils can develop dictionaries of special terms like *My Science Dictionary* or *My Health Dictionary.* From these they can advance to beginning and intermediate dictionaries.

This section deals mainly with the role the dictionary plays in helping children with word recognition; Part II of the primer discusses the dictionary as an aid to comprehension of word meanings.

Although the dictionary is undeniably useful in determining the pronunciation of unfamiliar words, students should turn to it only as a last resort for this purpose. They should consult it only after they have applied phonics and structural analysis clues along with knowledge of context clues. There are two major reasons for following this procedure. First, applying the appropriate word recognition skills immediately, without having to take the time to look up the word in the dictionary, is less of a disruption of the reader's train of thought and therefore less of a hindrance to comprehension. Second, a dictionary is not always readily available; thoroughly mastered word recognition skills, however, will always be there when they are needed.

When using other word attack skills has produced no useful or clear result, children should turn to the dictionary for help. Obviously, before children can use the dictionary for pronunciation, they must be able to locate words in it.

After children have located particular words, they need two more skills to pronounce the words correctly: the ability to interpret phonetic respellings and to interpret accent marks.

Interpreting Phonetic Respellings and Accent Marks

The pronunciation key, along with knowledge of sounds ordinarily associated with single consonants, helps in interpreting phonetic respellings in dictionaries. A pronunciation key is present somewhere on every page spread of a good dictionary. Students should not be asked to memorize the diacritical (pronunciation) markings used in a given dictionary, because different dictionaries use different markings; learning the markings for one could cause confusion when students use another. The sounds ordinarily associated with relatively unvarying consonants may or may not be included in the pronunciation key. Because they are not always included, it is important that children have a knowledge of phonics.

Here are four activities related to interpretation of phonetic spellings.

Activities

1. Have the students locate a given word in their dictionaries (example: *cheat* [*chēt*]). Call attention to the phonetic respelling beside the entry word. Point out the location of the pronunciation key and explain its function. Have the children locate each successive sound-symbol in the key—*ch, ē, t.* (If necessary, explain why the *t* is not included in the key.) Have the children check the key word for each symbol to confirm its sound value. Then have them blend the three sounds together to form a word. Repeat with other words. (Start with short words and gradually work up to longer ones.)

2. Code an entire paragraph or a joke using phonetic respellings. Provide a pronunciation key. Let groups of children compete to see who can write the selection in the traditional way first. Let each group of students who believe they have done so come to your desk. Check their work. If it is correct, keep it and give it a number indicating the order in which it was finished. If it is incorrect, send the students back to work on it some more. Set a time limit for the activity. The activity may be carried out on a competitive or a noncompetitive basis.

3. Give the children a pronunciation key, and let them encode messages to friends. Check the accuracy of each message before it is passed on to the friends to be decoded.

4. Use an activity such as the following Model Activity.

Model Activities

Pronunciation Key

Write the following hypothetical pronunciation key on the board. Tell the children: "Pretend that this list of words is part of the pronunciation key for a dictionary. Choose the key word or words that would help you pronounce each of the words listed below it. Hold up your hand when you have written the number of the appropriate key word on your paper beside the number of each entry word." (You may form the list of words from a book the children are about to read, thereby giving them some advance preparation for the words that they will meet in the book.)

When all the children have made their choices, call on a volunteer to reply to each one, telling why he or she chose a particular answer.

Pronunciation Key: (1) cat, (2) āge, (3) fär, (4) sōfə, (5) sit

1. cape (kāp)
2. car (kär)
3. ago (ə/gō′)
4. aim (ām)
5. fad (fad)
6. race (rās)
7. rack (rak)
8. affix (ə/fiks′)

Some words will have only one accent mark, whereas others will have marks showing different degrees of accent within a single word. Children need to be able to translate the accent marks into proper stress when they speak the words. Here are two ideas for use in teaching accent marks.

Activities

1. Write several familiar multisyllabic words on the board. (*Bottle* and *apartment* are two good choices.) Explain that when words of more than one syllable are spoken, certain syllables are stressed or emphasized by the speaker's breath. Pronounce each of the example words, pointing out which part or parts of each word receive stress. Next, tell the class that the dictionary uses accent marks to indicate which parts of words receive stress. Look up each word in the dictionary, and write the dictionary divisions and accent marks for the word on the board. Pronounce each word again, showing how the accent marks indicate the parts of the words that you stress when you pronounce them. Then have the children complete the following Model Activity.

2. Introduce the concept of accent in the same way described in the first activity. Then distribute sheets of paper with a list of words such as the following.

(1) des' ti na' tion

(2) con' sti tu' tion

(3) mys' ti fy'

(4) pen' nant

(5) thun' der storm'

Ask volunteers to read the words, applying the accents properly. When they have done so, give them a list of unfamiliar words with both accent marks and diacritical (pronunciation) marks inserted. (Lists will vary according to the children's ability. Use of words from their classroom reading material is preferable to use of random words.) Once again, ask the children to read the words, applying their dictionary skills.

Model Activities

Accent Marks

Write the following words on the board.

1. truth ful	6. peo ple
2. lo co mo tion	7. gig gle
3. fric tion	8. emp ty
4. at ten tion	9. en e my
5. ad ven ture	10. ge og ra phy

Call on volunteers to pronounce these words and decide where the accent is placed in each one.

Have them come to the board and indicate placements of the accents by putting accent marks (') after the syllables where they think the accents belong. Then have all the students look up the words in the dictionary and check the placements of the accents. Anyone who finds an incorrectly marked word can come to the board, make the correction, and pronounce the word with the accent correctly placed.

Word Recognition Procedure

It is helpful for children to know a strategy for decoding unfamiliar words independently. A child may discover the word at any point in the following procedure; he or she should then stop the procedure and continue reading. Sometimes it is necessary to try all of the steps.

Step 1. Apply context clues. This may involve reading to the end of the sentence or paragraph in which the word is found to intake enough context to draw a reasonable conclusion about the word.

Step 2. Try the sound of the initial consonant, vowel, or blend along with context clues.

Step 3. Check for structure clues (prefixes, suffixes, inflectional endings, compound words, or familiar syllables).

Step 4. Begin sounding out the word using known phonics generalizations. (Go only as far as necessary to determine the word.)

Step 5. Consult the dictionary.

A teacher may explain this five-step strategy in the following way:

1. First, try to decide what word might reasonably fit in the context in which you found the unfamiliar word. Ask yourself: "Will this word be a naming word? A word that describes? A word that shows action? A word that connects two ideas?" Also ask yourself: "What word will make sense in this place?" Do you have the answer? Are you sure of it? If so, continue to read. If not, go to Step 2.

2. Try the initial sound(s) along with the context clues. Does this help you decide? If you are sure you have the word now, continue reading. If not, go to Step 3.

3. Check to see if there are familiar word parts that will help you. Does the word have a prefix or suffix that you know? If this helps you decide on the word, continue reading. If not, go to Step 4.

4. Begin sounding out the word, using all of your phonics skills. If you discover the word, stop sounding and go back to your reading. If you have sounded out the whole word and it does not sound like a word you know, go to Step 5.

5. Look up the word in the dictionary. Use the pronunciation key to help you pronounce the word. If the word is one you have not heard before, check the meaning. Be sure to choose the meaning that fits the context.

For example, a reader who is confronted with the unfamiliar word *chamois* might apply the strategy in the following way:

1. "'He used a chamois to dry off the car.' I've never seen the word *c-h-a-m-o-i-s* before. Let's see. . . . Is it a naming word? . . . Yes, it is, because *a* comes before it. . . . What thing would make sense here? . . . It is something that can be used to dry a car. Could it be *towel*? . . . No, that doesn't have any of the right sounds. Maybe it is *cloth*? . . . No, *cloth* starts with *cl*."

2. "*Ch* usually sounds like the beginning of *choice*. . . . I can't think of anything that starts that way that would fit here. . . . Sometimes it sounds like *k*. . . . I can't think of a word that fits that either. . . . *Ch* even sounds like *sh* sometimes. . . . The only word I can think of that starts with the *sh* sound and fits in the sentence is *sheet*, and I can tell that none of the other sounds are right."

3. "I don't see a prefix, suffix, or root word that I recognize, either."

4. "Maybe I can sound it out. *Chămois*. No, that's not a word. *Kămois*. That's not a word either. *Shămois*. I don't think so. . . . Maybe the *a* is long. *Chāmois*. No. *Kāmois*. No. *Shāmois*. No."

5. "I guess I'll have to use the dictionary. What? *Shăm' ē*? Oh, I know what that is. I've seen Dad use one! Why is it spelled so funny? Oh, I see! It came from French."

A crucial point for teachers to remember is that children should not consider use of word recognition skills important *only* during reading classes. They should apply these skills whenever they encounter an unfamiliar word, whether it happens during reading class, science class, a free reading period, or in out-of-school situations. Teachers should emphasize to their students that the strategy explained here is applicable to *any* situation in which an unfamiliar word occurs.

Teachers should also encourage students to self-correct their reading errors when the words they read do not combine to make sense. This can be accomplished with some well-planned instruction. Taylor and Nosbush (1983) had children individually read orally from material at their instructional levels. They praised each child for things he or she did well when reading, especially any self-correcting behavior the student exhibited when miscues (unexpected responses) affected the meaning. They encouraged each student to try to make sure the material being read made sense. They also discussed some miscues that the student did not self-correct, particularly ones that did not make sense but for which good context clues were available. Students instructed in this way did better at self-correction than did students who read orally without being asked to pay attention to meaning.

Summary of Part I

Word recognition skills help readers identify words while reading. One skill is sight word recognition, the development of a store of words a person can recognize immediately on sight. Use of context clues to help in word identification involves using the surrounding words to decode an unfamiliar word. Both semantic and syntactic clues can be helpful. Phonics, the association of speech sounds (phonemes) with printed symbols (graphemes), is very helpful in identifying unfamiliar words, even though the sound-symbol associations in English are not completely consistent. Structural analysis skills enable readers to decode unfamiliar words using units larger than single graphemes. The process of structural analysis involves recognition of prefixes, suffixes, inflectional endings, contractions, and compound words, as well as syllabication and accent. Dictionaries can also be used for word identification. The dictionary respelling that appears in parentheses after the word supplies the word's pronunciation, but the reader has to know how to use the dictionary's pronunciation key to interpret the respellings appropriately.

Children need to learn to use all of the word recognition skills. Because they will need different skills for different situations, they must also learn to use the skills appropriately.

An overall strategy for decoding unfamiliar words is useful. The following five-step strategy is a good one to teach: (1) use context clues; (2) try the sound of the initial consonant, vowel, or blend in addition to context clues; (3) check for structure clues; (4) use phonics generalizations to sound out as much of the word as necessary; and (5) consult the dictionary.

Test Yourself

True or False

_____ 1. It is wise to teach only a single approach to word attack.

_____ 2. All word recognition strategies are learned with equal ease by all children.

_____ 3. Sight words are words that readers recognize immediately without needing to resort to analysis.

_____ 4. The English language is noted for the regularity of sound-symbol associations in its written words.

_____ 5. Teaching a small store of sight words can be the first step in implementing an analytic approach to phonics instruction.

_____ 6. Early choices for sight words to be taught should be words that are extremely useful and meaningful.

_____ 7. Games with complex rules are good ones to use for practice with sight words.

_____ 8. Most practice with sight words should involve the words in context.

_____ 9. If teachers teach phonics well, they do not need to bother with other word recognition strategies.

_____ 10. Consonant letters are more consistent in the sounds they represent than vowel letters are.

_____ 11. Phonics generalizations often have numerous exceptions.

_____ 12. It is impossible to teach too many phonics rules, since these rules are extremely valuable in decoding unfamiliar words.

_____ 13. In a word that has only one vowel letter at the end, the vowel letter usually represents its long sound.

_____ 14. It is wise to teach only one phonics generalization at a time.

_____ 15. Structural analysis skills include the ability to recognize prefixes and suffixes.

_____ 16. The addition of a prefix to a root word can change the word's meaning.

_____ 17. Inflectional endings can change verb tenses.

_____ 18. The apostrophe in a contraction indicates possession or ownership.

_____ 19. Every syllable contains a vowel sound.

_____ 20. There is only one vowel letter in each syllable.

_____ 21. Open syllables end in consonant sounds.

_____ 22. The vowel sound in an open accented syllable is usually long.

_____ 23. The schwa sound is often found in unaccented syllables.

_____ 24. When dividing words into syllables, we treat consonant blends and consonant digraphs as units and do not divide them.

_____ 25. Prefixes and suffixes generally form separate syllables.

_____ 26. Prefixes and suffixes are usually accented.

_____ 27. Picture clues are the most useful word recognition clues for sixth-grade students.

_____ 28. A comparison or contrast found in printed material may offer a clue to the identity of an unfamiliar word.

_____ 29. Context clues used by themselves provide only educated guesses about the identities of unfamiliar words.

_____ 30. Children should be expected to memorize the diacritical markings used in their dictionaries.

_____ 31. Accent marks indicate which syllables are stressed.

_____ 32. Some words have more than one accented syllable.

_____ 33. Writing new words is helpful to some learners in building sight vocabulary.

_____ 34. The language experience approach is good for developing sight vocabulary.

_____ 35. One method of teaching sight words is best for all students.

Multiple Choice

_____ 1. In the word *myth,* the *y*
   a. has the characteristics of a vowel.
   b. is silent.
   c. has the characteristics of a consonant.

_____ 2. When it occurs in the initial position in a syllable, the letter *w*
   a. stands for a vowel sound.
   b. is silent.
   c. stands for a consonant sound.

_____ 3. In the word *strong,* the letters *str*
   a. represent a consonant blend.
   b. are silent.
   c. represent a single sound.

_____ 4. Consonant digraphs
  a. represent two blended speech sounds.
  b. represent a single speech sound.
  c. are always silent.

_____ 5. The word *sheep* is made up of
  a. five sounds.
  b. four sounds.
  c. three sounds.

_____ 6. In the word *boat,* the *oa* is a
  a. vowel digraph.
  b. diphthong.
  c. blend.

_____ 7. In the word *boy,* the *oy* is a
  a. vowel digraph.
  b. consonant digraph.
  c. diphthong.

_____ 8. The word *diphthong* contains
  a. three consonant blends.
  b. three consonant digraphs.
  c. a consonant digraph and two consonant blends.

_____ 9. In the word *know,* the *ow* is a
  a. diphthong.
  b. vowel digraph.
  c. consonant blend.

_____ 10. In the word *his,* the letter *s* has the sound usually associated with the letter(s)
  a. *s.*
  b. *z.*
  c. *sh.*

_____ 11. Which type of accent mark indicates the heaviest emphasis?
  a. Primary
  b. Secondary
  c. Tertiary

For your journal...

1. Write a description of how you would teach sight recognition of function words that do not represent concrete images, words such as *for* and *which.*

2. React to the following statement: "Going back to teaching basic phonics skills will cure all of our country's reading ills."

3. After observing a teacher teaching a synthetic phonics lesson and a teacher teaching an analytic phonics lesson, write an evaluation of the two approaches, based upon your observations. Be sure to evaluate the methods, not the instructors.

4. React to the following statement: "I do not believe in teaching children to use context clues. It just produces a group of guessers."

...And your portfolio

1. Plan a lesson to teach one or more word recognition strategies, using a popular picture book that contains appropriate examples of phonic and structural analysis elements.

2. Develop a collection of rhymes, riddles, and poems to use to promote auditory discrimination skills.

Being able to decode words is an essential part of the reading process, but not enough in many cases to allow the reader to get meaning from the text. The next part of this primer, *Part II: Meaning Vocabulary*, deals with ways to enhance children's abilities to understand word meanings, thereby enabling them to improve their reading comprehension.

II Meaning Vocabulary

SETTING OBJECTIVES

When you finish reading Part II, you should be able to

▶ Discuss some factors involved in vocabulary development.

▶ Name and describe several techniques of vocabulary instruction.

▶ Identify some special types of words and explain how they can cause problems for children.

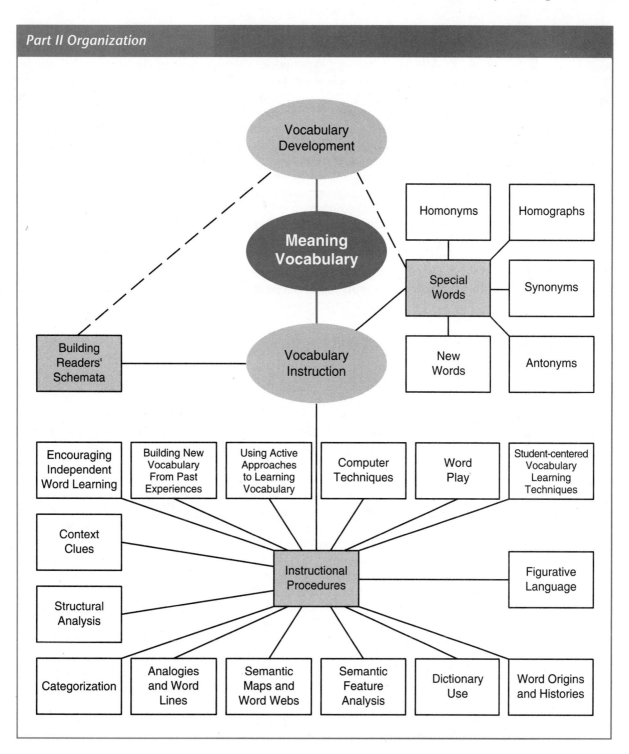

Part II Organization

Vocabulary Development

Meaning Vocabulary

Special Words

Homonyms

Homographs

Synonyms

Antonyms

New Words

Building Readers' Schemata

Vocabulary Instruction

Encouraging Independent Word Learning

Building New Vocabulary From Past Experiences

Using Active Approaches to Learning Vocabulary

Computer Techniques

Word Play

Student-centered Vocabulary Learning Techniques

Context Clues

Structural Analysis

Instructional Procedures

Figurative Language

Categorization

Analogies and Word Lines

Semantic Maps and Word Webs

Semantic Feature Analysis

Dictionary Use

Word Origins and Histories

M*eaning vocabulary* (words for which meanings are understood) is essentially the set of labels for the clusters of concepts that people have learned through experience. These clusters of concepts, or knowledge structures, are called *schemata*. Because students must call on their existing schemata in order to comprehend, meaning vocabulary development is an important component of comprehension (Jones, 1982). Therefore, direct instruction in word meanings is a valuable part of reading instruction. Research indicates that preteaching new vocabulary terms can result in significant gains in comprehension (Roser and Juel, 1982; Carney et al., 1984) and that long-term vocabulary instruction, in which words are taught and reinforced over a period of time, enhances comprehension of materials containing those words (Beck, Perfetti, and McKeown, 1982; McKeown et al., 1983; Robinson et al., 1990).

In Part I of this primer we examined the importance of decoding words and developing a sight vocabulary, but these abilities have little value if students do not understand the words. Children's sight vocabularies should be built from words they already comprehend, words that are a part of their meaning vocabularies. Part II focuses on the development of extensive meaning vocabularies and the difficulties that certain types of words may present to youngsters.

Vocabulary Development

It is difficult to pinpoint the age at which children learn the precise meanings of words. Early in the language development process, they learn to differentiate between antonyms (opposites), making more discriminating responses as they grow older. Sometimes they overgeneralize about word meanings: a very young child who learns the word *car,* for example, may apply it to any motor vehicle, making no discrimination among cars, trucks, vans, and other kinds of vehicles. Some children as old as nine years have trouble distinguishing between the meanings of *ask* and *tell,* and some children as old as ten years have not yet differentiated between the words *brother* and *boy* and the words *sister* and *girl* (McConaughy, 1978). As children mature, they learn more about choosing specific words.

Children increase their vocabularies at a rapid rate during the elementary school years. Vocabulary building is a complex process involving many kinds of words: words with *multiple meanings* (The candy is *sweet*. Mary has a *sweet* disposition.); words with *abstract definitions* (*Justice* must be served.); *homonyms* (She will take the *plane* to Lexington. He has on *plain* trousers.); *homographs* (I will *read* the newspapers. I have *read* the magazine.); *synonyms* (Marty was *sad* about leaving. Marty was *unhappy* about leaving.); and *antonyms* (Bill is a *slow* runner. Mary is a *fast* runner.). Children must also acquire meanings for a number of relational terms, such as *same/different, more/less, taller/shorter, older/younger, higher/lower,* and so on. In content area instruction, students must deal with *technical vocabulary* (words whose only meanings are specific to the content areas, for example, *photosynthesis*) and *specialized vocabulary* (words with general meanings as well as specialized meanings that are specific to the content area, for example, *pitch* in the area of music). Content area materials also abound with special *symbols* and *abbreviations* that children must master in order to read the materials successfully.

Vocabulary Instruction

Children learn much vocabulary by listening to the conversations of those around them. Therefore, a language-rich environment promotes vocabulary acquisition (Anderson and Nagy, 1991). Teachers can provide such environments in their classrooms. They can greatly influence children's vocabulary development simply by being good models of vocabulary use. For example, when teachers read aloud or give explanations to the class, they should discuss any new words used and encourage the children to use them. Teachers should not "talk down" to children but should use appropriate terminology in describing things to them and participating in discussions with them.

Learning new vocabulary may just involve acquisition of a new label for a concept that is already known. In this case, the teacher's task is simple. The teacher provides the new term (such as *journey*) and tells the children it means the same thing as a familiar term (such as *trip*) (Armbruster and Nagy, 1992).

Most teachers recognize the importance of vocabulary instruction as a part of reading and language arts classes. The importance of teaching word meanings and encouraging variety in word choice and exactness in expressing thoughts is generally accepted. Teachers therefore usually give attention to many aspects of vocabulary instruction—such as structural analysis; use of context clues; and use of reference books, such as dictionaries and thesauruses—during language classes. During these lessons, teachers also need to help the children understand the real-world purpose for building vocabulary: a rich vocabulary helps us to communicate effectively. The more words we know and use appropriately, the better we are able to communicate our knowledge and our feelings to others.

Vocabulary instruction should take place throughout the day, however, not just during the language arts or reading period. Vocabulary knowledge is important in all subject areas covered in the curriculum. Children need to develop their vocabularies in every subject area so that the specialized or technical words they encounter are not barriers to learning. Nelson-Herber (1986) suggests intensive direct teaching of vocabulary in specific content areas to help students read the content materials successfully. She endorses building from the known to the new, helping students understand the interrelationships among words in concept clusters (groups of related concepts), and encouraging students to use new words in reading, writing, and speaking. Construction of word meaning by the students from context, experience, and reasoning is basic to her approach. At times the students work in cooperative groups on vocabulary exercises, and they are involved with vocabulary learning before, during, and after reading of assigned material. The techniques described in Part II will help teachers plan effectively for vocabulary instruction in various content areas.

Time for Reflection Whereas some teachers stress the need for vocabulary instruction throughout the day, others argue that such instruction logically belongs in a reading or language arts class. **What do *you* think?**

Choosing words to teach can be a problem for teachers. Blachowicz and Lee (1991) suggest choosing these terms from classroom reading materials. The terms should be central to the selections in which they appear. The teacher should activate prior knowledge related to the words before the reading begins and have students use the new vocabulary in postreading discussion. Words that students still do not understand well need further attention and elaboration. The students might use the words in retellings, dramatizations, or writings based on the story or selection for further experiences.

Teachers can approach vocabulary instruction in a variety of ways, but some vocabulary instructional techniques appear to be more effective than others. The most desirable instructional techniques are those that

1. Assist students in integrating the new words with their background knowledge.
2. Assist students in developing elaborated (expanded) word knowledge.
3. Actively involve students in learning new words.
4. Help students acquire strategies for independent vocabulary development.
5. Provide repetition of the words to build ready accessibility of their meanings.
6. Have students engage in meaningful use of the words (Carr and Wixson, 1986; Nagy, 1988; Blachowicz and Lee, 1991; Beck and McKeown, 1991).

We will now look at several common methods of vocabulary development.

Building Readers' Schemata

Vocabulary terms are labels for *schemata,* or the clusters of concepts each person develops through experience. Sometimes children cannot understand the terms they encounter in books because they do not know the concepts to which the terms refer. In this case, concept or schemata development involving the use of direct and vicarious experiences is necessary. Blachowicz (1985) affirms the importance of building a conceptual base for word learning.

A good technique for concept development is to offer as concrete an experience for the concept as possible. The class should then discuss the attributes of the concept. The teacher should give examples and nonexamples of the concept, pointing out the attributes that distinguish examples from nonexamples. Next, the students should try to identify other examples and nonexamples that the teacher supplies and give their reasons. Finally, the students should suggest additional examples and nonexamples.

For example, to develop the concept of *banjo,* the teacher could bring a banjo to class. The teacher would show it to the students, play it for them (or get someone to do so), and let them touch it and pluck or strum the strings. A discussion of its attributes would follow. The children might decide that a banjo has a circular body and a long neck, that it has a tightly stretched cover over the body, that it has strings, and that one can play music on it. The teacher might show the children pictures or real examples of a variety of banjos, some with five and some with four strings, and some with enclosed backs and some with open backs. Then the teacher might show the children a guitar, pointing out the differences in construction (different shape, different material forming the front of the instrument, different number of strings, etc.). The teacher might also show several other instruments, at first following the same procedure, then letting the students identify how they are different from and similar to banjos. The students can provide their own examples of banjos by bringing in pictures or actual instruments. They will note that, although there may be some variation in size and appearance, the essential attributes are present. They can also name and bring pictures or actual examples of instruments that are not banjos, such as harps, mandolins, or violins, and explain why these instruments do not fit the concept.

Concrete experiences for abstract concepts are difficult to provide, but the teacher can use approximations. For example, to develop the concept of *freedom,* the teacher can say, "You may play with any of the play equipment in the room for the next ten minutes, or you may choose not to play at all." After ten minutes have passed, the teacher can tell the class that they were given the freedom to choose their activity; that is, they were not kept from doing what they chose to do. The teacher may then offer several examples of freedom. One might be the freedom to choose friends. No one else tells the children who their friends have to be; they choose based on their own desires. The teacher should also offer several nonexamples of freedom, perhaps pointing out that during a game players are restrained by a set of rules and do not have the freedom to do anything they want to do. Then the teacher should ask the students to give examples of freedom and explain why these examples are appropriate. A student may suggest that the freedom we have in this country to say what we think about our leaders is a good example, because we are not punished for voicing our views. After several examples, the students will be asked for nonexamples. They may suggest that people in jail do not have freedom, because they cannot go where they wish or do what they wish. After students have offered a number of nonexamples, the teacher may ask them to be alert for examples and nonexamples of freedom in their everyday activities and to report their findings to the class. Some may discover that being "grounded" by their parents is a good nonexample of freedom.

Thelen (1986) indicates that meaningful learning is enhanced by teaching general concepts before specific concepts. In this way, the children have the schemata they need to incorporate new facts they encounter. Using this approach, the teacher presents the concept of *dog* before the concept of *poodle,* and the children thus have a prior pool of information to which they can relate the new information about *poodle.* Isabel Beck has stated that ownership of a word, or the ability to relate the word to an existing schema, is necessary for meaningful learning. In other words, students need to relate the word to information they already know. Semantic mapping and semantic feature analysis (discussed later in Part II) are two particularly good methods for accomplishing this goal.

Firsthand experiences, such as field trips and demonstrations, can help students associate words with real situations. These experiences can be preceded and followed up by discussion of the new concepts, and written accounts of the experiences can help students gain control of the new vocabulary. For example, a field trip can be preceded by a discussion of the work that is done at the target location. During the field trip, each activity the students witness can be explained as they watch. This explanation should include the proper terms for the processes and personnel involved. After the trip, the students can discuss the experience. They can make graphic displays of the new terms (see the sections on semantic maps and word webs), classify the new terms (see the section on categorization), make comparison charts for the words (see the section on semantic feature analysis), analyze the structure of the words (see the section on structural analysis), or manipulate the new terms in some other way. They may write individual summaries of the experience or participate in writing a class summary. They may wish to use reference books to expand their knowledge about some of the new things they have seen. All of these activities will build both the children's concepts and their vocabularies, thereby enhancing their comprehension of material containing this vocabulary.

Vicarious experiences can also help to build concepts and vocabulary. Audiovisual aids, such as pictures, films, filmstrips, records, and videotapes, can be used to illustrate words that students have encountered in reading and provide other words for discussion. Books such as thesauruses, children's dictionaries, and trade books about words are also useful sources of information about words.

Storytelling and story reading are good ways to provide vicarious experiences. Studies by Roe (1985, 1986) and Pigg (1986) showed that a seven-week program of daily one-hour storytelling/story reading sessions with language follow-up activities could improve vocabulary skills of kindergarten, first-grade, and second-grade students. Students in the experimental groups in these studies produced more words in stories, more different words, and more multisyllabic words than students in the control groups did. Language follow-up activities included creative dramatics, creative writing (or dictation), retelling stories with the flannel board, and illustrating scenes from the stories and describing them to the teacher. The following Classroom Scenario is drawn from one of Roe's experiences.

**Classroom
Scenario**

Using Literature Selections to Develop Vocabulary

Dr. Roe (1985), a visiting teacher, was presenting the song "The Old Woman Who Swallowed a Fly" in a first-grade class. After she sang the line "How absurd to swallow a bird," she asked the students, "What does *absurd* mean?" None of them knew.

Dr. Roe told them that *absurd* meant *silly* or *ridiculous*. Then she asked them, "Would it be silly for a woman to swallow a bird?"

The children answered, "Yes," in unison.

"Would it be absurd for me to wear a flowerpot on my head to teach the class?" she then asked.

Again the children answered, "Yes!"

"What are some other absurd things that you can think of?" Dr. Roe finally asked.

Each child gave a reply. If the reply showed understanding of the term, Dr. Roe provided positive reinforcement. If it did not show understanding of the term, her questioning led the child to see why the thing mentioned was not absurd, and the child was given another chance to answer.

Weeks later, when these children encountered the word again in the story *Horton Hatches the Egg,* they remembered its meaning.

Analysis of Scenario

The children encountered a word in the context of a familiar song. The word's meaning was unclear to them, so the teacher supplied both a definition and other examples of the concept behind the term. To ensure that the children really understood the term, the teacher asked them to supply their own examples. This activity helped the children make the word their own through active involvement with it.

Instructional Procedures

Although procedures for vocabulary development vary widely, many of them have produced good results, and teachers should be familiar with a variety of approaches. A number of the programs described here combine several approaches, and good teachers will also use combinations of approaches in their classrooms. Graves and Prenn (1986) point out that "there is no one best method of teaching words . . . various methods have both their costs and their benefits and will be very appropriate and effective in some circumstances and less appropriate and effective in others" (p. 597).

Research on vocabulary instruction indicates that "extensive reading can increase vocabulary knowledge, but direct instruction that engages students in construction of word meaning, using context and prior knowledge, is effective for learning specific vocabulary and for improving comprehension of related materials" (Nelson-Herber, 1986, p. 627). McKeown and colleagues (1985) also offer support for this assessment.

Some research findings indicate that "vocabulary instruction improves comprehension only when both definitions and context are given, and has the largest effect when a number of different activities or examples using the word in context are used" (Stahl, 1986, p. 663). Techniques requiring students to think deeply about a term and its relationships to other terms are most effective. Class discussion seems to make students think more deeply about words as they make connections between their prior knowledge and new information. Multiple presentations of information about a word's meaning and multiple exposures to the word in varying contexts both benefit comprehension. In addition, the more time spent on vocabulary instruction, the better the results. Vocabulary programs that extend over a long period of time give students a chance to encounter the words in a number of contexts and to make use of them in their own language (Stahl, 1986).

When commercial materials are used, word meanings should be related to the students' own experiences through discussion. Then students should use the words in some way to demonstrate their understanding of the meanings. Because multiple experiences with each word are necessary for complete learning, the number of words presented should not be overwhelming. Spaced reviews of the words will enhance retention of the word meanings.

We will now look at a number of carefully researched instructional techniques and the studies related to them. Then we will describe several common methods of vocabulary development.

Using Active Approaches to Learning Vocabulary

Beck and McKeown (1983) described a program of vocabulary instruction that emphasized relating vocabulary to students' preexisting word knowledge and experiences. Students generated their own context for the terms being taught by answering questions about the words (for example, the teacher might say, "Tell about something you might want to *eavesdrop* on" [p. 624]). The program also helped students to further their word knowledge by introducing new words in global semantic categories, such as *people* or *places,* and by requiring the students to work with the relationships among words. The children were asked to differentiate among critical features of words and to generalize from one word to similar ones. They were also asked to complete analogies involving the words and to pantomime words. These activities were in keeping with suggestions 2 and 3 about effective vocabulary instructional techniques presented earlier; the students were active participants in the activities described rather than passive observers. Students were given a number of exposures to each word in a variety of contexts. The final aspect of the program was development of rapid responses to words by using timed activities, some of which were gamelike. These activities kept the students actively involved and probably increased their interest as well.

The children involved in Beck and McKeown's program learned the words taught, developed speed and accuracy in making semantic decisions, showed comprehension of stories containing the target words superior to that of a control group, and evidently learned more than the specific words taught, as indicated by the size of their gains on a standardized measure of reading comprehension and vocabulary.

A closely related procedure, developed by Blachowicz (1986), also helps teachers focus on vocabulary instruction. First, teachers activate what the students know about the target words in the reading selection, using either exclusion brainstorming (in which students exclude unrelated words from a list of possible associated words) or knowledge rating (in which students indicate their degree of familiarity with the words). Then the teachers can elicit predictions about "connections between words or between words and the topic and structure of the selection" (p. 644), emphasizing the words' roles in semantic networks. (Word webs or semantic feature analysis, discussed later in this chapter, may be used.) Next, the students are asked to construct tentative definitions of the words. They read the text to test these definitions, refining them as they discover additional information. Finally, the students use the words in other reading and writing tasks to make them their own.

Blachowicz (1985, p. 877) points out that "the harder one works to process stimuli . . . the better one's retention." Blachowicz's approach causes the students to work harder by predicting and constructing definitions rather than merely memorizing the material presented.

Another active way to clarify word meanings by associating situations with them is dramatization of words. This technique is more effective than mere verbal explanations of terms. Under some circumstances, dramatization of words has proved to be more effective than use of context clues, structural analysis, or dictionaries (Duffelmeyer, 1980; Duffelmeyer and Duffelmeyer, 1979).

Davis (1990) has pairs of students construct "concept cards" for new vocabulary terms. On the cards they list definitions, synonyms, and examples for the terms. She has the students supplement their own knowledge by consulting dictionaries and thesauruses. Then she has them discuss the various connotations of the synonyms provided. Following the discussion, the class is divided into teams that compete to supply the most definitions, synonyms, or examples for words from the cards.

Cudd and Roberts (1993/1994) use sentence expansion activities to work on vocabulary. They create sentence stems composed of syntactic structures and vocabulary the children have encountered in classroom reading materials. Then they display the stems on the board and lead a discussion of them. Students supply endings for the sentences and then read the completed sentences. Students write their sentences based on the stems, working with peer-editing partners. Then they illustrate one or two of their sentences. In this way, students become actively involved in using the target vocabulary.

Petrick (1992) suggests the use of manipulatives to explain or demonstrate content area vocabulary. Teachers can use tape measures to show the meanings of certain lengths (*foot, yard,* etc.), use cotton balls and water to demonstrate *absorption,* or use a rubber band to demonstrate the concept of *elasticity.*

Stahl and Kapinus (1991) found a technique called Possible Sentences to be effective in teaching content area vocabulary. In this activity, the teacher chooses six to eight difficult words and four to six familiar words that are important to the selection. The teacher writes these words on the board and may offer a definition of each one. Students are asked to supply possible sentences for these terms that include at least two of the words. This causes them to think about the relationships among the terms. When all words are represented in the possible sentences, the students read the selection. After reading, each possible sentence is discussed and either accepted as true or changed to make it true. This technique requires much active processing of the vocabulary.

Iwicki and her colleagues (1992) found that they could enhance vocabulary learning through an activity called Vocabulary Connections. They put the vocabulary terms and definitions on wall charts, then asked students to relate to each term situations in the literature selection they were reading and situations in previously read books. For example, the word *pandemonium* is used in *Welcome Home, Jelly Bean* (Shyer, 1988). It can later be related to events in *The Black Stallion* (Farley, 1941). This activity can be motivational and can encourage use of higher-level thinking skills.

Primary-grade children can be asked to illustrate new vocabulary words to show their understanding. Then the children's illustrations can be shown to a small group of other class members, who try to identify the word being illustrated in each picture and record it on their papers. Finally, each artist tells which word each of his or her pictures represented. This procedure gets the children very actively involved with words (Baroni, 1987).

Building New Vocabulary from Past Experiences

Word meaning should be taught from an experience base, to prevent students' acquiring a store of words for which they have only superficial understanding. Duffelmeyer (1985) suggests four techniques to link word meaning and experience: use of synonyms and examples, use of positive and negative instances of the concepts, use of examples and definitions, and use of definitions together with sentence completion. His techniques are all teacher directed and involve verbal interaction between the teacher and the students.

Encouraging Independent Word Learning

Instruction that gradually moves the responsibility for determining new word meanings from the teacher to the student helps students become independent learners. Teachers can guide students to use context clues to define words independently by using a four-part procedure. First, students are given categorization tasks. Second, they practice determining meanings from complete contexts. Third, they practice determining meaning in incomplete contexts. Finally, they practice defining new vocabulary by means of context clues (Carr and Wixson, 1986).

Context Clues

In Part I, we discussed the use of *context clues* to help children recognize words that are familiar in speech but not in print. Context clues can also key the meaning of an unfamiliar word by directly defining the word, providing an *appositive,* or comparing or contrasting the word with a known word. For example:

A *democracy* is a government run by the people being governed. (definition)

He made an effort to *alleviate,* or relieve, the child's pain until the doctor arrived. (appositive)

Rather than encountering hostile natives, as they had expected, many settlers found the natives to be *amicable.* (contrast)

Context can also offer clues in sentences other than the one in which the new word appears, so children should be encouraged to read surrounding sentences for clues to meaning. Sometimes an entire paragraph embodies the explanation of a term, as in the following example:

I've told you before that the flu is contagious! When Johnny had the flu, Beatrice played with him one afternoon, and soon Beatrice came down with it. Joey caught it from her, and now you tell me you have been to Joey's house. I hope you don't come down with the flu and have to miss the party on Saturday.

When introducing new words in context, teachers should use sentences that students can relate to their own experiences and that have only one unfamiliar word each. It is best not to use the new word at the very beginning of the sentence, since the children will not have had any of the facilitating context before they encounter it (Duffelmeyer, 1982).

Teachers can use a "think-aloud" strategy to help students see how to use context clues. Here is a sample activity that makes use of this strategy.

Model Activities

Intermediate-Level Lesson on Context Clues

Write one of the sentences mentioned previously on the board or display it using a transparency. Say: "Rather than encountering hostile natives, as they had expected, many settlers found the natives to be amicable. I wonder what *amicable* means? Let's see; the sentence says *'Rather than encountering hostile natives.'* That means the natives weren't hostile. *Hostile* means *unfriendly*; so maybe *amicable* means *friendly*."

After several example "think-aloud" activities in which the teacher models the use of context clues, the teacher can ask student volunteers to "think aloud" the context clues to specific words. Students may work in pairs on a context clues worksheet and verbalize their context usage strategies to each other. Finally, the students should work alone to determine meanings from context clues.

Blachowicz (1993) suggests a procedure called *C(2)QU* to teach context use. The steps are as follows:

C1: *Context.*   A broad, meaningful context is provided for an unfamiliar word. Students hypothesize about the meaning.

C2: *Context.*   More explicit context is provided. Students orally analyze their original hypotheses.

Q: *Question.*   Students are asked a question involving the meaning of the word. They discuss the meaning.

U: *Use.*   Students are asked to use the word appropriately in oral or written sentences.

This procedure requires active participation by students, which should result in more effective learning.

Context clues are available in both text and illustrations in many trade books, such as *The Amazing Bone* by William Steig (Farrar, Straus & Giroux, 1976). *A Gaggle of Geese,* by Eve Merriam (Knopf, 1960), puts collective terminology for groups into an interesting context (Howell, 1987). Teaching use of context clues in these meaningful settings encourages students to use such clues in their independent reading.

Some researchers have found that use of closed-caption television programs to provide readers with both auditory and visual context was effective with below-average readers and bilingual students (Koskinen et al., 1993; Neuman and Koskinen, 1992). They found that such programs provided readers with print to read in a motivational format. Words could be discussed while the students were viewing video images. Later they could be read from handouts prepared with sentences drawn from the captioned video and finally from magazines and books on the same topic. They could also be used in written retellings of the viewed episode. Although the match between the audio and the captions seen was not exact, the captions were presented at a rapid rate for poor readers (about 120 words per minute), and the captions were in all capital letters, the results teachers obtained were impressive. Videotaping the programs allows repetition of the reading for different purposes and use of small segments (only a few minutes each) of video in a lesson. However, copyright laws must be studied to ensure that use is in compliance with these laws.

Edwards and Dermott (1989) select difficult words from material about to be assigned, take a quotation using each word in good context from the material, and provide written comments to the students to help them use appropriate context clues or other strategies (primarily structural analysis or dictionary use). The students try to use the clues available to decide on the meanings of the words before reading. Class discussion helps the students to think through the strategy use.

Gipe (1980) expanded a context method (in which students read new words in meaningful contexts) to include having children apply the words based on their own experiences and then studied the effectiveness of this method, compared to three other methods. The other methods were an association method (in which an unknown word is paired with a familiar synonym), a category method (in which students place words in categories), and a dictionary method (in which students look up the word, write a definition, and use the word in a sentence). The expanded context method was found to be the most effective of the four. The application of the new words may have been the most important aspect of the context method that Gipe used. After the students derived the meaning of the

Students can consult dictionaries for meanings of words for which the context gives inadequate information. (© *Mary Kate Denny/Photo Edit*)

word from a variety of contexts, including a definition context, they *applied* the word to their personal experiences in a written response. Thus, the instruction follows the first desirable instructional technique for vocabulary listed earlier in this chapter: assisting students in integrating the new words with their background knowledge.

Teachers need to help students learn *why* and *when* to use context clues (Blachowicz and Zabroske, 1990). Context clues are useful when the context is explicit about word meaning, but they are less useful when the meaning is left unclear. If the clues are too vague, they may actually be misleading (Schwartz, 1988; Schatz and Baldwin, 1986). Furthermore, if the word is not important to understanding the passage, the explicitness of the context is not important. Teachers should model their decision-making processes about the importance of determining the meaning of the word, the usefulness of the context, and the kinds of clues available there through think-alouds. Students need to realize that the meanings they attribute to the words must pass the test inherent in the question "Does this make sense here?" They also need to realize that structural analysis clues may help them decide whether or not a meaning suggested by the context is reasonable.

It is estimated that average ten- to fourteen-year-old students could acquire from 750 to 8,250 new words each year through incidental, rather than directed, contextual learning (Schwartz, 1988; Herman et al., 1987; Nagy, Herman, and Anderson, 1985; Wysocki and Jenkins, 1987). Helping students learn to use context more efficiently should therefore greatly enhance their vocabulary learning.

Using a selection the students are about to read, take an unfamiliar word, put it into a title, and construct several sentences that offer clues to its meaning. Show the title on the overhead projector; then show one sentence at a time, letting the students guess the meaning of the word at each step (Kaplan and Tuchman, 1980).

Activities

Combining contextual and definitional approaches to vocabulary instruction is more effective than using a contextual approach alone. In fact, "it would be hard to justify a contextual approach in which the teacher did not finally provide an adequate definition of the word or help the class arrive at one" (Nagy, 1988, p. 8). In addition, teachers can have students apply context clues fruitfully in conjunction with structure clues, which we will discuss next.

Structural Analysis

Structural analysis, discussed in Part I as a word recognition skill, can also be used as an aid in discovering meanings of unknown words. Knowing meanings of common affixes and combining them with meanings of familiar root words can help students determine the meanings of many new words. For example, if a child knows the meaning of *joy* and knows that the suffix *-ous* means *full of,* he or she can conclude that the word *joyous* means *full of joy.* Students can often determine meanings of compound words by relating the meanings of the component parts to each other (*watchdog* means a *dog* that *watches*). After some practice, they can be led to see that the component parts of a compound word do not always have the same relationships to each other (*bookcase* means a *case* for *books*).

Children begin to learn about word structure very early. First, they deal with words in their simplest, most basic forms—as *morphemes,* the smallest units of meaning in a language. (The word *cat* is one morpheme.) Then they gradually learn to combine morphemes. If an *s* is added to form the plural, *cats,* the final *s* is also a morpheme, because it changes the word's meaning. There are two classes of morphemes, distinguished by function: *free* morphemes, which have independent meanings and can be used by themselves (*cat, man, son*), and *bound* morphemes, which must be combined with another morpheme to have meaning. Affixes and inflectional endings are bound morphemes; the *-er* in *singer* is an example.

Practice activities such as the following can help children see how prefixes and suffixes change meanings of words. *Un-* is the most common prefix appearing in the *Word Frequency Book* (Carroll, Davies, and Richman, 1971; White, Sowell, and Yanagihara, 1989).

**Model
Activities**

Prefix *un-*

Have the students read the book *Fortunately* by Remy Charlip (New York: Scholastic, 1964). Discuss with them the meanings of *fortunately* and *unfortunately,* using the situations from the book to make the discussion concrete and clear. When they have stated that *unfortunately* means *not fortunately* or *the opposite of fortunately,* have them decide what part of the word means *not.* After they identify the *un-* as the part that means *not,* have them name other words they know that begin with *un-.* Discuss the meanings of these words, pointing out that the prefix means *not* or *the opposite of* in each case in which the remainder of the word forms a root word, but not if the beginning two letters are not a prefix attached to a root word. Ask them to look in their reading assignments for words starting with *un-* in which *un-* is a prefix added to a root word. Have them use their knowledge of the meaning of *un-* to determine the meanings of each of these words.

White, Sowell, and Yanagihara (1989) caution teachers that prefixes may have more than one meaning. *Un-, re-, in-,* and *dis-,* the four most frequently used prefixes, have at least two meanings each. *Un-* and *dis-* may each mean either *not* or *do the opposite. In-* may mean either *not,* or *in,* or *into. Re-* may mean either *again* or *back.* Both the word parts and the context of the word should be considered in determining meanings of prefixed words.

The following Classroom Scenario shows another application of structural analysis in the classroom.

**Classroom
Scenario**

Use of Structural Analysis Skills

A middle school science textbook presented two theories of the solar system: a geocentric theory and a heliocentric theory. Two diagrams were provided to help the students visualize the two theories, but the diagrams were not labeled. Mrs. Brown, the teacher, asked the students, "Which diagram is related to each theory?"

Matt's hand quickly went up, and he accurately identified the two diagrams.

"How did you decide which was which?" asked Mrs. Brown.

"You told us that *geo-* means *earth. Centric* looks like it comes from *center.* This diagram has the earth in the center. So I decided it was geocentric. That would mean the other one was heliocentric. Since the sun is in the center in it, I guess *helio-* means *sun.*"

Analysis of Scenario

Mrs. Brown had taught an important science word part the first time it occurred in her class. She had encouraged her students to use their knowledge of word parts to figure out unfamiliar words. Matt followed her suggestions and managed to make decisions about key vocabulary based on his knowledge of word parts.

The students can study word cards that contain words derived from Latin or Greek word parts, such as *prescription* and *scripture.* They can be encouraged to think of other examples and asked to use the derived words in sentence context.

See the Focus on Strategies on Compound Words for an activity that can offer practice in determining meanings of compound words.

Focus on Strategies

Compound Words

Mr. Clay based his lesson on the book *The Seal Mother* by Mordicai Gerstein (Dial, 1986). He introduced the story by saying that it was an old Scottish folktale. He wrote the word *folktale* on the board. Then he asked, "What can you tell me about this word?"

Bobby said, "It is made up of two words: *folk* and *tale.* That makes it a compound word."

"Good, Bobby," Mr. Clay responded. "What does that make you believe this word means?"

"A tale is a story," LaTonya replied.

"That's right," said Mr. Clay. "Can anyone add anything else to what we know about the word's meaning? What does *folk* mean?"

Carl answered tentatively, "A kind of music?"

"There is folk music, just as there are folktales, but we still need a meaning for the word *folk*," Mr. Clay responded.

After he got only shrugs, he explained, "A folktale is a tale, or story, told by the folk, or common people, of a country. Folktales were passed down orally from older people to younger ones over the years. See how both parts of the compound word give something to the meaning?

"Listen as I read this story to you. When I finish, we will try to retell the story by listing the main events."

The children listened intently. When he finished the story, Mr. Clay asked them to list the events in the story in order. As they suggested events, he wrote each one on the board. When he had listed all of the events they could remember, they discussed how to put some of the events in the proper order. Mr. Clay erased and moved the sentences around until the children were satisfied.

Then Mr. Clay asked the children, "Did you use any compound words to retell the story?"

Hands shot up all over the room. Mr. Clay called on them one by one, and they pointed out *fisherman, sealskin, without, oilcloth, inside, rayfish, everywhere, grandfather,* and *whenever.* The children who mentioned the words were allowed to go to the board and circle them, identify the two words that made up each compound, and try to define each compound word, using the meanings of the two component words. Other students helped in determining the definitions, and sometimes the dictionary was consulted.

Finally, the children were asked to copy the compound words from the board into their vocabulary study notebooks. "I'm putting three copies of *The Seal Mother* in the reading center for the rest of this week," Mr. Clay said. "When you have time, take your vocabulary notebook to the center and read the book to yourself or with a partner. Each time you find one of our compound words, put a checkmark by the word in your notebook. When you find a compound word that we didn't use in our retelling, copy it into your notebook, and write a definition for it, using the meanings of the two words and the context of the sentence in which you found it. We'll discuss the other words that you found on Friday."

On Friday, the children had found a number of words in the book that they hadn't used in their retelling, including *moonlit, moonlight, everything, wide-eyed, tiptoed, another,* and *into.* A discussion of the words and their meanings followed. Mr. Clay asked how use of some of these words added to the children's understanding of the story.

"*Moonlit* and *moonlight* give you a picture in your mind of the scene," Jared said.

"*Wide-eyed* lets us know how his parents' talk made the boy feel," Marissa added.

"*Tiptoed* showed us how he walked quietly," Tyrone said.

"Watch for compound words in other books that you read, and use the meanings of the two words in each compound to help you with meanings that you don't already know," Mr. Clay told them as he ended the lesson.

Categorization

Categorization is grouping together things or ideas that have common features. Classifying words into categories can be a good way to learn more about word meanings. Young children can begin learning how to place things into categories by grouping concrete objects according to their traits. Once the children have developed some sight vocabulary, it is a relatively small step for them to begin categorizing the words they see in print according to their meanings. Very early in their instruction, children will be able to look at the following list and classify the words into such teacher-supplied categories as "people," "things to play with," "things to eat," and "things to do."

Word List

doll	bicycle	ball	run	girl
candy	cookie	boy	baby	sit
toy	dig	sing	mother	banana

The children may discover that they want to put a word in more than one category. This desire will provide an opportunity for discussion about how a word may fit in two or more places for different reasons. The children should give reasons for all of their placements.

After the children become adept at classifying words into categories supplied by the teacher, they are ready for the more difficult task of generating the categories needed for classifying the words presented. The teacher may give them a list of words such as the following and ask them to place the words in groups of things that are alike and to name the trait the items have in common.

Word List

horse	cow	goose	stallion	foal
gosling	mare	filly	chick	calf
colt	gander	bull	hen	rooster

Children may offer several categories for these words: various families of animals; four-legged and two-legged animals; feathered and furred animals; winged and wingless animals; or male animals, female animals, or animals that might be either sex. They may also come up with a classification that the teacher has not considered. As long as the classification system makes sense and the animals are correctly classified according to the stated system, it should be considered correct. Teachers should encourage students to discover various possibilities for classifications.

Discussion of the different classification systems may help to extend the children's concepts about some of the animals on the list, and it may help some children develop concepts related to some of the animals for the first time. The classification system allows them to relate the new knowledge about some of the animals to the knowledge they already have about these animals or others. The usefulness of categorization activities is supported by research indicating that presenting words in semantically related clusters can lead to improvement in students' vocabulary knowledge and reading comprehension (Marzano, 1984).

A classification game such as the one in the next Model Activity provides an interesting way to work on categorization skills.

Model Activities

Classification Game

Divide the children into groups of three or four, and make category sheets like the one shown here for each group. When you give a signal, the children start writing as many words as they can think of that fit in each category; when you signal that time is up, a child from each group reads the group's words to the class. Have the children compare their lists and discuss why they placed particular words in particular categories.

Appropriate categories other than the ones used below are meats, fruits, and vegetables; mammals, reptiles, and insects; or liquids, solids, and gases.

Cities	States	Countries

The ability to classify is a basic skill that applies to many areas of learning. Many of the other activities described in Part II, including those for analogies, semantic maps, and semantic feature analysis, depend on categorization.

Analogies and Word Lines

Analogies compare two relationships and thereby provide a basis for building word knowledge. Educators may teach analogies by displaying examples of categories, relationships, and analogies; asking guiding questions about the examples; allowing students to discuss the questions; and applying the ideas that emerge (Bellows, 1980).

Students may need help in grouping items into categories and understanding relationships among items. For example, the teacher might write *nickel, dime,* and *quarter* on the board and ask, "How are these things related? What name could you give the entire group of items?" (Answer: *money.*) Teachers can use pictures instead of words in the primary grades; in either case, they can ask students to apply the skill by naming other things that would fit in the category (*penny* and *dollar*). Or the teacher could write *painter* and *brush* and ask, "What is the relationship between the two items?" (Answer: A *painter* works with a *brush*.) Teachers should remember to simplify their language for discussions with young children and to have students give other examples of the relationship (*dentist* and *drill*). After working through many examples such as these, the students should be ready for examples of simple analogies, such as "Light is to dark as day is to night," "Glove is to hand as sock is to foot," and "Round is to ball as square is to block." Students can discuss how analogies work: "How are the first two things related? How are the second two things related? How are these relationships alike?" They can then complete incomplete analogies, such as "Teacher is to classroom as pilot is to _____." Younger children should do this orally; older ones can understand the standard shorthand form of *come:go::live:die* if they are taught to read the colon (:) as *is to* and (::) as *as* (Bellows, 1980).

HuffBenkoski and Greenwood (1995) taught second graders how to use analogies. These authors modeled their reasoning processes for the students through think-alouds as they analyzed analogies. They also had students explain their reasoning processes. The children came up with a definition for *analogies.* Attention then was given to classification activities—choosing words that did or did not belong with a given set of words related to a theme study. Next, the children were asked to state the relationship between two words. Following that, students completed analogies that had one part missing. Finally, students produced their own analogies in groups and individually.

Teachers may use word lines to show the relationships among words, just as they use number lines for numbers. They can arrange related words on a graduated line that emphasizes their relationships. For young children, they can use pictures and words to match or ask them to locate or produce appropriate pictures. Upper-grade students can be asked to arrange a specified list of words on a word line themselves. Word lines can concretely show antonym, synonym, and degree analogies, as in this example:

enormous	large	medium	small	tiny

Analogies that students could develop include "enormous is to large as small is to tiny" (synonym); "enormous is to tiny as large is to small" (antonym); and "large is to medium as medium is to small" (degree). The teacher can have the children make their own word lines and analogies (Macey, 1981).

Dwyer (1988) suggests mapping analogies, as shown in Example 2. This map provides the relationship involved, a complete example, two incomplete examples for the students to complete, and one space for an example that comes entirely from the student.

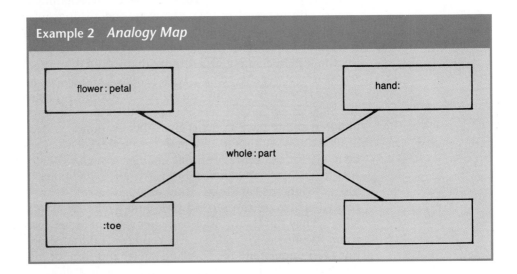

Example 2 *Analogy Map*

Semantic Maps and Word Webs

Semantic maps can be used to teach related concepts (Johnson and Pearson, 1984; Johnson, Pittelman, and Heimlich, 1986). "Semantic maps are diagrams that help students see how words are related to one another. . . . Students learn the meanings and uses of new words, see old words in a new light, and see relationships among words" (Heimlich and Pittelman, 1986).

To construct a semantic map with a class, the teacher writes on the board or a chart a word that represents a concept that is central to the topic under consideration. The teacher asks the students to name words related to this concept. The students' words are listed on the board or chart grouped in broad categories, and the students name the categories. They may also suggest additional categories. A discussion of the central concept, the listed words, the categories, and the interrelationships among the words follows.

The discussion step appears to be the key to the effectiveness of this method, because it allows the students to be actively involved in the learning. After the class has discussed the semantic map, the teacher can give an incomplete semantic map to the children and ask them to fill in the words from the map on the board or chart and add any categories or words that they wish. The children can work on their maps as they do the assigned reading related to the central concept. Further discussion can follow the reading, and more categories and words can be added to the maps. The final discussion and mapping allow the children to recall and graphically organize the information they gained from the reading (Johnson, Pittelman, and Heimlich, 1986; Stahl and Vancil, 1986). Example 3 shows a semantic map constructed by one class.

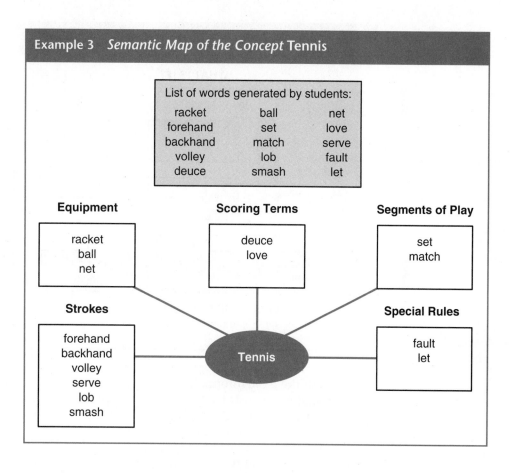

Example 3   *Semantic Map of the Concept* Tennis

List of words generated by students:

racket	ball	net
forehand	set	love
backhand	match	serve
volley	lob	fault
deuce	smash	let

Equipment
racket
ball
net

Scoring Terms
deuce
love

Segments of Play
set
match

Strokes
forehand
backhand
volley
serve
lob
smash

Tennis

Special Rules
fault
let

Because a semantic map shows both familiar and new words under labeled categories, the process of constructing one helps students make connections between known and new concepts (Johnson, Pittelman, and Heimlich, 1986). The graphic display makes relationships among terms easier to see. Discussion of the map allows the teacher to assess the children's background knowledge, clarify concepts, and correct misunderstandings (Stahl and Vancil, 1986).

Schwartz and Raphael (1985) used a modified approach to semantic mapping to help students develop a concept of *definition.* The students learned what types of information are needed for a definition and learned how to use context clues and background knowledge to help them better understand words. Word maps are really graphic representations of definitions. The word maps Schwartz and Raphael used contained information about the general class to which the concept belonged, answering the question "What is it?"; the properties of the concept, answering the question "What is it like?"; and examples of the concept (see Example 4).

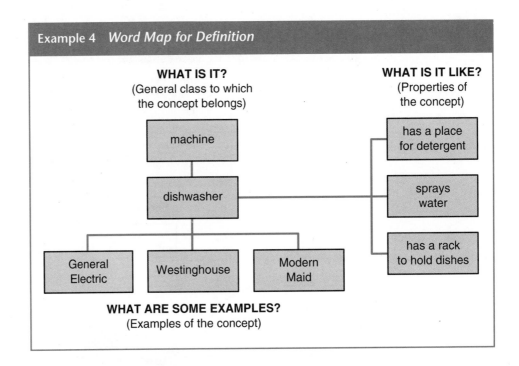

Example 4 *Word Map for Definition*

WHAT IS IT?
(General class to which the concept belongs)

WHAT IS IT LIKE?
(Properties of the concept)

machine

dishwasher

has a place for detergent

sprays water

has a rack to hold dishes

General Electric

Westinghouse

Modern Maid

WHAT ARE SOME EXAMPLES?
(Examples of the concept)

With the basic information contained in such a map, students have enough information to construct definitions. This procedure for understanding the concept of definition is effective from the fourth-grade level through college. The approach used by Schwartz and Raphael started with strong teacher involvement, but control was gradually transferred to the children. Children were led to search the context of a sentence in which the word occurred for the elements of definition needed to map a word. Eventually the teachers provided only partial context for the word, leading the children to go to outside sources, such as dictionaries, for information to complete the maps. Finally, teachers asked the students to write definitions, including all the features previously mapped, without actually mapping the word on paper. This activity helps bring meanings of unknown terms into focus through analogies and examples (Smith, 1990).

Word webs are another way to represent the relationships among words graphically. Students construct these diagrams by connecting related words with lines. The words used for the web may be taken from material students have read in class.

Semantic Feature Analysis

Semantic feature analysis is a technique that can help children understand the uniqueness of a word as well as its relationships to other words (Johnson and Pearson, 1984). To perform such an analysis, the teacher lists in a column on the board or a chart some known words with common properties. Then the children generate a list of features possessed by the various items in the list. A feature only needs to apply to one item to be listed. The teacher writes these features in a row across the top of the board or chart, and the students fill in the cells of the resulting matrix with pluses to indicate the presence of the feature and minuses to indicate its absence.

Example 5 shows a partial matrix developed by children for various buildings. "Walls" and "doors" were other features the children suggested for the matrix; they were omitted from the example only for space considerations. Both of these features received a plus for each building, emphasizing the similarities of the terms *jail, garage, museum,* and *church.*

Example 5	*Semantic Feature Analysis Chart*							
	barred windows	exhibits	steeple	cross	cars	lift-up doors	guards	oil stains
jail	+	–	–	–	–	–	+	–
garage	?	–	–	–	+	+	–	+
museum	?	+	–	–	?	–	+	–
church	–	–	+	+	–	–	–	–

The children discussed the terms as they filled in the matrix. In the places where the question marks occur, the children said, "Sometimes it may have that, but not always. It doesn't have to have it." The group discussion brought out much information about each building listed and served to expand the children's existing schemata.

Students can continue to expand such a matrix after initially filling it out by adding words that share some of the listed features. For example, the children added *grocery store* to the list of buildings in Example 5 because it shared the walls and doors, and they added other features showing the differentiation, such as *food, clerks,* and *shopping carts.*

Johnson and Pearson (1984) suggest that after experience with these matrices, children may begin to realize that some words have different degrees of the same feature. At this time, the teacher may want to try using a numerical system of coding, using 0 for *none,* 1 for *some,* 2 for *much,* and 3 for *all.* Under the feature "fear," for example, *scared* might be coded with a 1, whereas *terrified* might be coded with a 3.

Anders and Bos (1986) suggest using semantic feature analysis with vocabulary needed for content area reading assignments. They believe that, because the analysis activates the students' prior knowledge through discussion and relates prior knowledge to new knowledge, students will have increased interest in the reading and therefore will learn more. This technique can be used before, during, and after the reading. A chart can be started in the background-building portion of the lesson, added to or modified by the students as they read the material, and refined further during the follow-up discussion of the material.

Metaphoric or figurative language (nonliteral language) can also be taught through a technique similar to semantic feature analysis (Thompson, 1986). A comparison chart can clarify differences and similarities between concepts that are not literally members of the same category. Finding similarities between essentially dissimilar things helps children understand the comparisons used in metaphoric language. For example, both *eyes* and *stars* might have the characteristic "shining" or "bright," leading to the source of the intended comparison in the expression "her eyes were like stars." (A detailed section on figurative language appears later in Part II.)

Dictionary Use

The dictionary can be an excellent source for discovering meanings of unfamiliar words, particularly for determining the appropriate meanings of words that have multiple definitions or specific, technical definitions. In some instances, children may be familiar with several common meanings of a word, but not with a word's specialized meaning found in a content area textbook. For example, a child may understand a reference to a *base* in a baseball game but not a discussion of a military *base* (social studies material), a *base* that turns litmus paper blue (science material), or *base* motives of a character (literature). Words that have the greatest number of different meanings, such as *run* or *bank,* are frequently very common.

Dictionaries are not always used properly in schools, however. Teachers should instruct children to consider the context surrounding a word, read the different dictionary definitions, and choose the definition that makes the most sense in the context. Without such instruction, children have a strong tendency to read only the first dictionary definition and to try to force it into the context. The teacher should model the choice of the correct definition for the students so that they can see what the task is. Students will then need to practice the task under teacher supervision.

The following Model Activities, pages 93 and 94, are good to use for practice immediately following instruction in dictionary use and for later independent practice.

In order to use the dictionary properly for vocabulary development, students must be instructed to consider a word's context, to read the different definitions, and to choose a definition for the word in its specific context. (© *Ed Lettau/Photo Researchers*)

Students can also use dictionaries to study *etymology,* the origin and history of words. Dictionaries often give the origin of a word in brackets after the phonetic respelling (although not all dictionaries do this in the same way), and archaic or obsolete definitions are frequently given and labeled so that students can see how words have changed.

Appropriate Dictionary Definitions

Model Activities

Write the following sentences on the board. Ask the children to find the dictionary definition of *sharp* that fits each sentence. You may ask them to jot each definition down and have a whole-class or small-group discussion about each one after all meanings have been located, or you may wish to discuss each meaning as it is located. The students may read other definitions for *sharp* in the dictionary and generate sentences for these as well.

1. Katherine's knife was very sharp.

2. There is a sharp curve in the road up ahead.

3. Sam is a sharp businessman. That's why he has been so successful.

4. I hope that, when I am seventy, my mind is as sharp as my grandmother's is.

5. We are leaving at two o'clock sharp.

Multiple Meanings of Words

Model Activities

Give the students a list of sentences, drawn from their textbooks, that contain words with specialized meanings for that subject. Have them use the dictionary or the textbook's glossary to discover the specialized meanings that fit the context of the sentences. After the students have completed the task independently, go over the sentences with them and discuss reasons for right and wrong responses.

The material you give to the students may look something like this:

Directions: Some words mean different things in your textbooks from what they mean in everyday conversation. In each of the following sentences, find the special meanings for the words and write these meanings on the lines provided.

1. Frederick Smith has decided to *run* for mayor. _____

2. The park was near the *mouth* of the Little Bear River. _____ _____

3. The management of the company was unable to avert a *strike.* _____ _____

4. That song is hard to sing because of the high *pitch* of several notes. _____

5. That number is written in *base* two. _____ _____

Teaching word meanings through dictionary use has been widely criticized, but it is nevertheless a useful technique for vocabulary development if it is applied properly. Research (e.g., Graves and Prenn, 1986) supports this view. Combining a definitional approach to vocabulary instruction with a contextual approach is more effective than using a definitional approach in isolation. Sentences that illustrate meanings and uses of the defined words can help immensely (Nagy, 1988).

Word Origins and Histories

As mentioned earlier, the study of word origins and histories is called *etymology.* Children in the intermediate grades will enjoy learning about the kinds of changes that have taken place in the English language by studying words and definitions that appear in very old dictionaries and by studying differences between American English and British English. Following is an additional useful source: Funk, Wilfred. *Word Origins & Their Romantic Stories.* Avenal, New Jersey: Outlet Book Company, 1992.

Teachers need to help children understand the different ways words can be formed. *Portmanteau* words are formed by merging the sounds and meanings of two different words (for example, *smog,* from *smoke* and *fog*). *Acronyms* are words formed from the initial letters of a name or by combining initial letters or parts from a series of words (for example, *radar,* from *ra*dio *d*etecting *a*nd *r*anging). Some words are just shortened forms of other words (for example, *phone,* from *telephone; flu,* from *influenza;* and *piano,* from *pianoforte*). Both shortened forms and acronyms are ways our language has become more compact (Richler, 1996). Some words are borrowed from other languages (for example, *lasso,* from the Spanish *lazo*). The teacher can discuss the origins of such terms when they occur in students' reading materials. In addition, students should try to think of other words that have been formed in a similar manner. The teacher may also wish to contribute other examples from familiar sources.

Figurative Language

Figurative language, or nonliteral language, can be a barrier to understanding written selections. Children tend to interpret literally many expressions that have meanings different from the sums of the meanings of the individual words. For example, the expression "the teeth of the wind" does not mean that the wind actually has teeth, nor does "a blanket of fog" mean a conventional blanket. Context clues indicate the meanings of such phrases in the same ways that they cue the meanings of individual words.

Adults often assume children have had exposure to expressions that in fact are unfamiliar to them. Children need substantial help in order to comprehend figurative language. Even basal readers present many of these expressions. Some common figures of speech that cause trouble are

1. *Simile*—a comparison using *like* or *as*

2. *Metaphor*—a direct comparison without the words *like* or *as*

3. *Personification*—giving the attributes of a person to an inanimate object or abstract idea

4. *Hyperbole*—an extreme exaggeration

5. *Euphemism*—substitution of a less offensive term for an unpleasant term or expression

Teaching children to recognize and understand similes is usually not too difficult, because the cue words *like* and *as* help to show the presence of a comparison. Metaphors, however, may cause more serious problems. A metaphor is a comparison between two unlike things that share an attribute (Readence, Baldwin, and Head, 1986). Sometimes children do not realize that the language in metaphors is figurative; sometimes they do not have sufficient background knowledge about one or both of the things being compared; and sometimes they simply have not learned a process for interpreting metaphors.

The two things compared in a metaphor may seem to be incompatible, but readers must think of past experiences with each, searching for a match in attributes that could be the basis of comparison. Visual aids can be helpful in this process. Thompson (1986) suggests a comparison chart like the following.

Comparison Chart

Man	*Mouse*
–	small
–	squeaks
√	alive
–	four legs
√+	timid

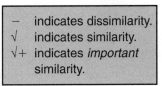

> – indicates dissimilarity.
> √ indicates similarity.
> √+ indicates *important* similarity.

The teacher can "think aloud" about the operation of metaphors and their purposes, asking students questions related to the process being demonstrated. Group discussion of the comparison chart helps to activate students' prior knowledge about the items being compared, and the chart helps make similarities more obvious.

Readence, Baldwin, Rickelman, and Miller (1986) found specific word knowledge to be an important factor in interpreting metaphors. The traditional practice offered in many commercial materials may not be helpful to students in interpreting other metaphors not covered in the material. Readence, Baldwin, and Head (1986, 1987) suggest the following instructional sequence for teaching metaphorical interpretation:

1. The teacher can display a metaphor, such as "Her eyes were stars," together with the more explicit simile, "Her eyes were as bright as stars," and explain that metaphors have missing words that link the things being compared (such as *bright* does). Other sentence pairs can also be shown and explained.

2. Then the students can be asked to find the missing word in a new metaphor, such as "He is a mouse around his boss." They can offer guesses, explaining their reasons aloud.

3. The teacher can explain that people have lists of words related to different topics stored in their minds. Examples can be modeled by the teacher and then produced by the students. At this point, the students can try to select the attribute related to the new metaphor. If there are two incorrect guesses, the attribute *timid* can be supplied and the reason for this choice given. This process can then be repeated with another metaphor.

4. As more metaphors are presented, the teacher can do less modeling, turning over more and more control of the process to the students.

After explaining each type of figurative language, modeling its interpretation, and having students interpret it under supervision, the teacher may provide independent practice activities such as the following ones. Ideally, the teacher should take examples of figurative expressions from literature the children are currently reading and use these expressions in constructing practice activities.

Activities

1. Show students pictures of possible meanings for figurative expressions found in their reading materials, and ask them to accept or reject the accuracy of each picture. Have them look carefully at the context in which the expression was found before answering. (For example, if you illustrate the sentence "She worked like a horse" with a woman pulling a plow, children should reject the picture's accuracy.)

2. Give each child a copy of a poem that is filled with figures of speech, and have the class compete to see who can "dig up" all the figures of speech first. You may require students to label all figures of speech properly as to type and to explain them.

Teachers can also use an activity like the Model Activity below to illustrate figures of speech.

Model Activities

Figures of Speech

Display the following cartoon on a transparency:

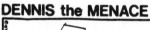

DENNIS the MENACE

"I hear you been through the mill....what do they **DO** there?'

Lead a discussion about the cartoon using the following questions as a guide.

1. What does "been through the mill" really mean, as Dennis's mother used it?

2. What does Dennis think it means?

3. How is the woman likely to react to Dennis's question?

4. How does Dennis's mother probably feel about the question?

5. Can misunderstanding figurative language cause trouble at times? Why do you say so?

Have the children suggest other figurative expressions that could produce misunderstandings. Then, as a follow-up activity, let them draw funny scenes in which the misunderstandings occur.

Also have the children look for other examples in newspaper comics. Ask them to cut out the examples and bring them to school for discussion.

DENNIS THE MENACE® used by permission of Hank Ketcham and © by Field Enterprises, Inc.

Student-Centered Vocabulary Learning Techniques

Some vocabulary learning techniques focus on students and their individual needs and interests. Explanations of several of these techniques follow.

Vocabulary Self-Collection Strategy. Haggard (1986) suggests the following approach for general vocabulary development:

1. Ask each child to bring to class a word that the entire class should learn. (The teacher brings one, too.) Each child should determine the meaning of his or her word from its context, rather than looking it up in the dictionary.

2. Write the words on the board. Let each participant identify his or her word and tell where it was found, the context-derived meaning, and why the class should learn the word. The class should then discuss the meaning of the word, in order to clarify and extend it and to construct a definition on which the class agrees. The result may be checked against a dictionary definition, if desired.

3. Narrow the list down to a manageable number, and have the students record the final list of words and definitions in their vocabulary journals. Some students may want to put eliminated words on their personal lists.

4. Make study assignments for the words.

5. Test the students on the words at the end of the week.

Word Banks or Vocabulary Notebooks. Students can form their own word banks by writing on index cards words they have learned, their definitions, and sentences showing the words in meaningful contexts. They may also want to illustrate the words or include personal associations or reactions to the words. Students can carry their word banks around and practice the words in spare moments, such as while waiting for the bus or the dentist. In the classroom, the word banks can be used in word games and in classification and other instructional activities.

Vocabulary notebooks are useful for recording new words found in general reading or words heard in conversations or on radio or television. New words may be alphabetized in the notebooks and defined, illustrated, and processed in much the same way as word bank words.

Both word banks and vocabulary notebooks can help children maintain a record of their increasing vocabularies. Generally, word banks are used in primary grades and notebooks in intermediate grades and above, but there are no set limits for either technique.

Word Play

Word play is an enjoyable way to learn more about words. It can provide multiple exposures to words in different contexts that are important to complete word learning. Gale (1982, p. 220) states, "Children who play with words show a stronger grasp of meaning than those who do not. To create or comprehend a pun, one needs to be aware of the multiple meanings of a word."

The following activities present some other ways that teachers can engage children in word play.

Activities

1. Have students write words in ways that express their meanings; for example, they may write *backward* as *drawkcab,* or *up* slanting upward and *down* slanting downward.

2. Ask them silly questions containing new words. Example: "Would you have a terrarium for dinner? Why or why not?"

3. Discuss what puns are and give some examples. Then ask children to make up or find puns to bring to class. Let them explain the play on words to classmates who do not understand it. Example: "What is black and white and read all over?" Answer: A newspaper (word play on the homonyms *red* and *read*).

4. Use Hink Pinks, Hinky Pinkies, and Hinkety Pinketies—rhyming definitions for terms with one, two, and three syllables, respectively. Give a definition, tell whether it is a Hink Pink, Hinky Pinky, or Hinkety Pinkety, and let the children guess the expression. Then let the children make up their own terms. Several examples follow.

   Hink Pink: Unhappy father—Sad dad

   Hinky Pinky: Late group of celebrators—Tardy party

   Hinkety Pinkety: Yearly handbook—Annual manual

5. Give the students a list of clues ("means the same as . . . ," "is the opposite of . . . ," and so forth) to words in a reading selection, along with page numbers. Tell them to go on a scavenger hunt for the words and write the words beside the appropriate clues (Criscuolo, 1980).

6. Have students use what Ruddiman (1993) calls the "Vocab Game" to develop students' word knowledge. For this game, have each student bring in a word from real-life reading each week. Have the students try to stump you with their words, while other students try to figure out their classmates' words. In the process, affixes and roots are located, dictionary definitions checked, the contexts in which the words were found shared, synonyms and antonyms discussed, and analogies presented. The class can earn points by stumping you or by figuring out another student's word. Have a recorder keep a record of the information about the words, which you word process and duplicate for the class. Use cloze-type tests (teacher or student constructed) to check the learning of the vocabulary.

7. Students might also enjoy crossword puzzles or hidden-word puzzles that highlight new words in their textbooks or other instructional materials.

Riddles are a very effective form of word play. To use riddles, children must interact verbally with others; to create riddles, they have to organize information and decide on significant details. Riddles can help children move from the literal to the interpretive level of understanding (Gale, 1982). Tyson and Mountain (1982) point out that riddles provide both context clues and high-interest material. Both of these factors promote vocabulary learning.

Riddles can be classified into several categories: those based on homonyms, on rhyming words, on double meanings, and on figurative/literal meanings, for example. (See the section "Special Words" later in this *Primer*.) An example of a homonym riddle is: "What does a grizzly *bear* take on a trip? Only the *bare* essentials" (Tyson and Mountain, 1982, p. 170).

Riddles work best with children who are at least six years old (Gale, 1982), and they continue to be especially effective with children through eleven years of age. After that, interest in this form of word play wanes.

Time for Reflection	Some people think word play is a waste of time. Others say it aids vocabulary development. **What do *you* think?**

Computer Techniques

Computers are present in many elementary school classrooms in this age of high technology, and the software available includes many programs for vocabulary development. Although some of them are simply drill-and-practice programs, which are meant to provide practice with word meanings the teacher has already taught, some tutorial programs provide initial instruction in word meanings. (These programs may also include a drill-and-practice component.) Programs focusing on synonyms, antonyms, homonyms, and words with multiple meanings are available, as are programs providing work with classification and analogies.

Word-processing programs that have a find-and-replace function can be profitably used in vocabulary instruction. A child may be given a disk that has files containing paragraphs with certain words used repeatedly. The child may use the find-and-replace function to replace all instances of a chosen word with a synonym and then read the paragraph to see if the synonym makes sense in each place it appears. If it does not, the child can delete the synonym in the inappropriate places and choose more appropriate replacements for the original word or actually put the original word back into the file. Then the child can read the file again to see if the words chosen convey the correct meanings and if the variation in word choices makes the paragraph more interesting to read.

A paragraph such as the following one could be a starting place:

Shonda had to run to the store for her mother because, just before the party, her mother got a run in her pantyhose. Shonda had to listen to her mother run on and on about her run of bad luck that day before she was able to leave the house. When she arrived at the store, she saw her uncle, who told her he had decided to run for office, delaying her progress further. She finally bought the last pair of pantyhose in the store. There must have been a run on them earlier in the day.

Time for Reflection	Some teachers think that having students learn the dictionary definitions of weekly teacher-chosen vocabulary words is a good approach to vocabulary instruction. Others believe in using a variety of methods to help students acquire meaning vocabulary. **What do *you* think?**

Special Words

Special types of words, such as those discussed in the following sections, need to be given careful attention.

Homonyms

Homonyms (also known as *homophones*) can cause trouble for young readers because they are spelled differently but pronounced the same way. Some common homonyms are found in the following sentences.

I want to *be* a doctor.
That *bee* almost stung me.

She has *two* brothers.
Will you go *to* the show with me?
I have *too* much work to do.

I can *hear* the bird singing.
Maurice, you sit over *here*.

Mark has a *red* scarf.
Have you *read* that book?

I *ate* all of my supper.
We have *eight* dollars to spend.

Fred Gwynne's *A King Who Rained* (Windmill, 1970) and *A Chocolate Moose for Dinner* (Windmill/Dutton, 1976) both have homonyms in their titles, as well as throughout their texts (Howell, 1987). Pettersen (1988) suggests letting the students look for homonyms in all of their reading materials. Students can construct lists of homonym pairs that mean something to them because they discovered the qualifying words for at least one word in each pair themselves. This paragraph is a good one to use as a starter for such an exercise, if readers want to try it for themselves. (Hint: *all-awl* is a good start.) Expanding Pettersen's activity to require the use of each homonym in a meaningful sentence is a way to keep the focus on meaning.

Activities

1. Have children play a card game to work on meanings of homonyms. Print homonyms on cards and let the children take turns drawing from each other, as in the game of Old Maid. A child who has a pair of homonyms can put them down if he or she gives a correct sentence using each word. The child who claims the most pairs wins.

2. Have students web homonyms in the following way:

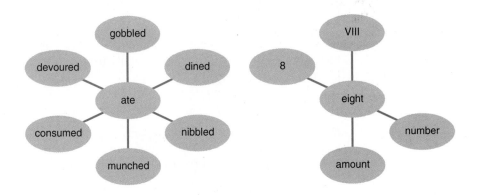

Homographs

Homographs are words that have identical spellings but not the same meanings. Their pronunciations may or may not be the same. Readers must use context clues to identify the correct pronunciations, parts of speech, and meanings of homographs. Examples include:

I will *read* my newspaper. (pronounced *rēd)*
I have *read* my newspaper. (pronounced *rĕd)*

I have a *contract* signed by the president. (noun: pronounced *con' trakt;* means a document)
I didn't know it would *contract* as it cooled. (verb: pronounced *cən/trakt';* means to reduce in size)

The books by Fred Gwynne mentioned in the section on homonyms are also rich sources of homographs.

Synonyms

Synonyms are words that have the same or very similar meanings. Work with synonyms can help expand children's vocabularies.

Study of the sports page of the newspaper for ways that writers express the ideas of *win* and *lose* can be a good way to introduce synonyms. The teacher should take this opportunity to show the students the different shadings of meaning that synonyms may have. For example, the headlines "Cats Maul Dogs" and "Cats Squeak By Dogs" both mean that the Cats beat the Dogs, but one indicates a win by a large margin, whereas the other indicates a close game. In addition, some synonyms are on varying levels of formality (for example, *dog* and *pooch*) (Breen, 1989).

Sylvester and the Magic Pebble by William Steig (Simon & Schuster, 1969) offers several good opportunities for discussion of synonyms used in describing the rain's cessation, the lion's movement, and the lion's feelings. In *Alexander and the Terrible, Horrible, No Good, Very Bad Day* by Judith Viorst (Atheneum, 1972), the synonyms are right there in the title, ready for discussion (Howell, 1987).

A teacher can also provide a stimulus word and have the students find as many synonyms as they can. The class can discuss the small differences in meaning of some words suggested as synonyms. For example, the teacher can ask, "Would you rather be called *pretty* or *beautiful*? Why?"

Antonyms

Antonyms are two words that have opposite meanings. Their meanings are not merely different; they are balanced against each other on a particular feature. In the continuum *cold, cool, tepid, warm,* and *hot,* for example, *cold* is the opposite of *hot,* being as close to the extreme in a negative direction as *hot* is in a positive direction. Thus, *cold* and *hot* are antonyms. *Tepid* and *hot* are different, but not opposites. *Cool* and *warm* are also antonyms. Similarly, *buy* and *sell* are antonyms because one is the reverse of the other. But *buy* and *give* are not antonyms, because no exchange of money is involved in the giving. The words are different, but not opposite. Powell (1986) points out that the use of opposition (citing antonyms) in defining terms can help to set the extremities of a word's meaning and provide its shadings and nuances. Research has shown that synonym production is helped by antonym production, but the reverse has not been shown to be true. Therefore, work with antonyms may enhance success in synonym exercises.

Frog and Toad Are Friends by Arnold Lobel (Harper & Row, 1970) provides students with examples of antonyms to discuss in an interesting context (Howell, 1987). Teachers may wish to locate other trade books that could be used for meaningful exposures to antonyms.

New Words

New words are constantly being coined to meet the changing needs of society and are possible sources of difficulty. Have students search for such words in their reading and television viewing and then compile a dictionary of words so new that they are not yet in standard dictionaries. The class may have to discuss these words to derive an accurate definition for each one, considering all the contexts in which the students have heard or seen it (Koeller and Khan, 1981). These new words may have been formed from Latin and Greek word elements, from current slang, or by shortening or combining older words (Richek, 1988).

Summary of Part II

Acquiring a meaning vocabulary involves developing labels for the schemata, or organized knowledge structures, that a person possesses. Because vocabulary is an important component of reading comprehension, direct instruction in vocabulary can enhance reading achievement. Although pinpointing the age at which children learn the precise meanings of words is difficult, children generally make more discriminating responses about word meanings as they grow older, and vocabulary generally grows with increasing age.

There are many ways to approach vocabulary instruction. The best techniques link new terms to the children's background knowledge, help them expand their word knowledge, actively involve them in learning, help them become independent in acquiring vocabulary, provide repetition of the words, and have them use the words meaningfully. Techniques that cause children to work harder to learn words tend to aid retention. Teachers may need to spend time on schema development before working with specific vocabulary terms.

Vocabulary development should be emphasized throughout the day, not just in reading and language classes; children can learn much vocabulary from the teacher's modeling of vocabulary use. Context clues, structural analysis, categorization, analogies and word lines, semantic maps and word webs, semantic feature analysis, dictionary use, study of word origins and histories, study of figurative language, a number of student-centered learning techniques, word play, and computer techniques can be helpful in vocabulary instruction.

Some special types of words can cause comprehension problems for children. They include homonyms, homographs, synonyms, antonyms, and newly coined words.

Test Yourself

True or False

_____ 1. Context clues are of little help in determining the meanings of unfamiliar words, although they are useful for recognizing familiar ones.

_____ 2. Structural analysis can help in determining meanings of new words containing familiar prefixes, suffixes, and root words.

_____ 3. When looking up a word in the dictionary to determine its meaning, a child needs to read only the first definition listed.

_____ 4. Homonyms are words that have identical, or almost identical, meanings.

_____ 5. Antonyms are words that have opposite meanings.

_____ 6. Word play is one good approach to building vocabulary.

_____ 7. Children sometimes make overgeneralizations in dealing with word meanings.

_____ 8. The development of vocabulary is essentially a child's development of labels for his or her schemata.

_____ 9. Work with analogies bolsters word knowledge.

_____ 10. Semantic mapping involves systematically deleting words from a printed passage.

_____ 11. Instruction in vocabulary that helps students relate new terms to their background knowledge is helpful.

_____ 12. Active involvement in vocabulary activities has little effect on vocabulary learning.

_____ 13. Pantomiming word meanings is one technique to produce active involvement in word learning.

_____ 14. Children should have multiple exposures to words they are expected to learn.

_____ 15. Working hard to learn words results in better retention.

_____ 16. There is no one best way to teach words.

_____ 17. Both concrete and vicarious experiences can help to build concepts.

_____ 18. Vocabulary instruction should receive attention during content area classes.

_____ 19. "Think-aloud" strategies can help students see how to use context clues.

_____ 20. Although use of categorization activities is motivational, according to current research findings it is not an effective approach.

_____ 21. Semantic mapping can help students develop a concept of definition.

_____ 22. Semantic feature analysis is the same thing as structural analysis.

_____ 23. Semantic feature analysis can help students see the uniqueness of each word studied.

_____ 24. The study of word origins is called _etymology._

_____ 25. Word banks can help students maintain a record of their increasing vocabularies.

_____ 26. At present no computer programs are available for vocabulary development.

_____ 27. A word-processing program can facilitate certain types of vocabulary instruction.

_____ 28. Children instinctively understand figures of speech; therefore, figurative language presents them with no special problems.

For your journal...

1. Reflect on the value of context clues for vocabulary development.

2. React to commercial computer software for vocabulary development that you have used. Include strengths and weaknesses of the programs.

...And your portfolio

1. Plan a lesson on dictionary use that requires the students to locate the meaning of a word that fits the context surrounding that word.

2. Plan a lesson designed to teach the concept of *justice* to a group of sixth grade students.

3. After collecting examples of figurative language from a variety of sources, use them as the basis for a lesson on interpreting figurative language.

Primer Summary

This primer has focused on word recognition and vocabulary skills that are essential for creating independent readers. Without these basic skills, young readers will lack the prerequisites for becoming proficient readers as they progress through school. The focus of Part I is on decoding, or simply learning how to recognize and identify words. Part II builds on Part I by suggesting ways to help children derive meaning from words, perhaps by relating them to personal experiences, categorizing them, or discovering relationships among them. It is important to realize, however, that these two parts are dependent on each other and should be integrated as much as possible during instruction. Word recognition should be taught in meaningful contexts, and children should pay close attention to the phonetic and structural make-up of words as they add new ones to their vocabularies. A strong foundation in word recognition and meaning vocabulary will support students through the years in their growth toward reading proficiency.

Answers to "Test Yourself"

Part I   True-False

1. F	13. T	25. T
2. F	14. T	26. F
3. T	15. T	27. F
4. F	16. T	28. T
5. T	17. T	29. T
6. T	18. F	30. F
7. F	19. T	31. T
8. T	20. F	32. T
9. F	21. F	33. T
10. T	22. T	34. T
11. T	23. T	35. F
12. F	24. T	

Part II   True-False

1. F	11. T	21. T
2. T	12. F	22. F
3. F	13. T	23. T
4. F	14. T	24. T
5. T	15. T	25. T
6. T	16. T	26. F
7. T	17. T	27. T
8. T	18. T	28. F
9. T	19. T	
10. F	20. F	

Part I   Multiple Choice

1. a	5. c	9. b
2. c	6. a	10. b
3. a	7. c	11. a
4. b	8. b	

Bibliography

Adams, Marilyn Jager. *Beginning to Read: Thinking and Learning about Print.* Cambridge, Mass.: MIT Press, 1990.

Adams, Marilyn Jager, et al. *"Beginning to Read:* A Critique by Literacy Professionals and a Response by Marilyn Jager Adams." *The Reading Teacher,* 44 (February 1991), 370–395.

Anders, Patricia L., and Candace S. Bos. "Semantic Feature Analysis: An Interactive Strategy for Vocabulary Development and Text Comprehension." *Journal of Reading,* 29 (April 1986), 610–616.

Anderson, Nancy A. "Teaching Reading as a Life Skill." *The Reading Teacher,* 42 (October 1988), 92.

Anderson, Richard C., Elfrieda H. Hiebert, Judith A. Scott, and Ian A. G. Wilkinson. *Becoming a Nation of Readers: The Report of the Commission on Reading.* Washington, D.C.: National Institute of Education, 1985.

Anderson, Richard C., and William E. Nagy. "Word Meanings." In *Handbook of Reading Research, Volume II,* edited by Rebecca Barr, Michael L. Kamil, Peter Mosenthal, and P. David Pearson. New York: Longman, 1991, pp. 690–724.

Armbruster, Bonnie B., and William E. Nagy. "Vocabulary in Content Area Lessons." *The Reading Teacher,* 45 (March 1992), 550–551.

Ashton-Warner, Sylvia. *Teacher.* New York: Simon & Schuster, 1963.

Bailey, Mildred Hart. "The Utility of Phonic Generalizations in Grades One Through Six." *The Reading Teacher,* 20 (February 1967), 413–418.

Ball, E. W., and B. A. Blachman. "Does Phoneme Awareness Training in Kindergarten Make a Difference in Early Word Recognition and Developmental Spelling?" *Reading Research Quarterly,* 26, no. 1 (1991), 49–66.

Baroni, Dick. "Have Primary Children Draw to Expand Vocabulary." *The Reading Teacher,* 40 (April 1987), 819–820.

Beck, I., and C. Juel. "The Role of Decoding in Learning to Read." *American Educator,* 8 (Summer 1995), 8–23.

Beck, I. L., C. A. Perfetti, and M. G. McKeown. "Effects of Long-Term Vocabulary Instruction on Lexical Access and Reading Comprehension." *Journal of Educational Psychology,* 74 (1982), 506–521.

Beck, Isabel L., and Margaret G. McKeown. "Learning Words Well—A Program to Enhance Vocabulary and Comprehension." *The Reading Teacher,* 36 (March 1983), 622–625.

Beck, Isabel L., and Margaret G. McKeown. "Research Directions: Social Studies Texts Are Hard to Understand: Mediating Some of the Difficulties." *Language Arts,* 68 (October 1991), 482–490.

Bellows, Barbara Plotkin. "Running Shoes Are to Jogging as Analogies Are to Creative/Critical Thinking." *Journal of Reading,* 23 (March 1980), 507–511.

Blachowicz, Camille L. Z. "C(2)QU: Modeling Context Use in the Classroom." *The Reading Teacher,* 47 (November 1993), 268–269.

Blachowicz, Camille L. Z. "Making Connections: Alternatives to the Vocabulary Notebook." *Journal of Reading,* 29 (April 1986), 643–649.

Blachowicz, Camille L. Z. "Vocabulary Development and Reading: From Research to Instruction." *The Reading Teacher,* 38 (May 1985), 876–881.

Blachowicz, Camille L. Z., and John J. Lee. "Vocabulary Development in the Whole Literacy Classroom." *The Reading Teacher,* 45 (November 1991), 188–195.

Blachowicz, Camille L. Z., and Barbara Zabroske. "Context Instruction: A Metacognitive Approach for At-Risk Readers." *Journal of Reading,* 33 (April 1990), 504–508.

Bradley, L., and P. Bryant. "Categorizing Sounds and Learning to Read—A Causal Connection." *Nature,* 301 (1983), 419–421.

Breen, Leonard. "Connotations." *Journal of Reading,* 32 (February 1989), 461.

Bristow, Page Simpson. "Are Poor Readers Passive Readers? Some Evidence, Possible Explanations, and Potential Solutions." *The Reading Teacher,* 39 (December 1985), 318–325.

Bruck, Maggie, and Rebecca Treiman. "Learning to Pronounce Words: The Limitations of Analogies." *Reading Research Quarterly,* 27, no. 4 (1992), 374–388.

Burmeister, Lou E. "Usefulness of Phonic Generaliza-tions." *The Reading Teacher,* 21 (January 1968): 349–356, 360.

Carney, J. J., D. Anderson, C. Blackburn, and D. Bless-ing. "Preteaching Vocabulary and the Comprehension of Social Studies Materials by Elementary School Children." *Social Education,* 48 (1984), 71–75.

Carnine, Douglas W. "Phonics Versus Look-Say: Transfer to New Words." *The Reading Teacher,* 30 (March 1977), 636–640.

Carr, Eileen, and Karen K. Wixson. "Guidelines for Evalu-ating Vocabulary Instruction." *Journal of Reading,* 29 (April 1986), 588–595.

Carroll, John B., Peter Davies, and Barry Richman. *The American Heritage Word Frequency Book.* Boston: Houghton Mifflin, 1971.

Ceprano, Maria A. "A Review of Selected Research on Methods of Teaching Sight Words." *The Reading Teacher,* 35 (December 1981), 314–322.

Clay, M. M. *The Early Detection of Reading Difficulties,* 3d ed. Auckland, New Zealand: Heinemann, 1993.

Clymer, Theodore. "The Utility of Phonic Generalizations in the Primary Grades." *The Reading Teacher,* 50 (November 1996), 182–187.

Cordts, Anna D. *Phonics for the Reading Teacher.* New York: Holt, Rinehart and Winston, 1965.

Criscuolo, Nicholas P. "Creative Vocabulary Building." *Journal of Reading,* 24 (December 1980), 260–261.

Cudd, Evelyn T., and Leslie L. Roberts. "A Scaffolding Technique to Develop Sentence Sense and Vocabulary." *The Reading Teacher,* 47 (December 1993/January 1994), 346–349.

Cunningham, Patricia M. "A Compare/Contrast Theory of Mediated Word Identification." *The Reading Teacher,* 32 (April 1979), 774–778.

Cunningham, Patricia M. "Decoding Polysyllabic Words: An Alternative Strategy." *The Reading Teacher,* 21 (April 1978), 608–614.

Cunningham, Patricia M. *Phonics They Use: Words for Reading and Writing.* New York: HarperCollins, 1991.

Cunningham, Patricia M., and James W. Cunningham. "Making Words: Enhancing the Invented Spelling-Decod-ing Connection." *The Reading Teacher,* 46 (October 1992), 106–115.

Daneman, Meredyth. "Individual Differences in Reading Skills." In *Handbook of Reading Research, Vol. II,* edited by R. Barr, M. L. Kamil, P. Mosenthal, and P. D. Pearson. New York: Longman, 1991, pp. 512–538.

Davis, Susan J. "Synonym Rally: A Vocabulary Concept Game." *Journal of Reading,* 33 (February 1990), 380.

DeSerres, Barbara. "Putting Vocabulary in Context." *The Reading Teacher,* 43 (April 1990), 612–613.

Downing, John. "How Children Think about Reading." In *Psychological Factors in the Teaching of Reading,* compiled by Eldon E. Ekwall. Columbus, Ohio: Charles E. Merrill, 1973.

Duffelmeyer, Frederick A. "The Influence of Experience-Based Vocabulary Instruction on Learning Word Mean-ings." *Journal of Reading,* 24 (October 1980), 35–40.

Duffelmeyer, Frederick A. "Introducing Words in Con-text." *The Reading Teacher,* 35 (March 1982), 724–725.

Duffelmeyer, Frederick A. "Teaching Word Meaning from an Experience Base." *The Reading Teacher,* 39 (October 1985), 6–9.

Duffelmeyer, Frederick A., and Barbara Blakely Duf-felmeyer. "Developing Vocabulary Through Dramatiza-tion." *Journal of Reading,* 23 (November 1979), 141–143.

Edwards, Anthony T., and R. Allan Dermott. "A New Way with Vocabulary." *Journal of Reading,* 32 (March 1989), 559–561.

Ehri, L. C., and C. Robbins. "Beginners Need Some Decoding Skill to Read Words by Analogy." *Reading Research Quarterly,* 27, no. 1 (1992), 13–26.

Emans, Robert. "The Usefulness of Phonic Generalizations Above the Primary Grades." *The Reading Teacher,* 20 (Febru-ary 1967), 419–425.

Fry, Edward. *Elementary Reading Instruction.* New York: McGraw-Hill, 1977.

Gale, David. "Why Word Play?" *The Reading Teacher,* 36 (November 1982), 220–222.

Gaskins, I. W., L. C. Ehri, C. Cress, C. O'Hara, and K. Donnelly. "Analyzing Words and Making Discoveries about the Alphabetic System: Activities for Beginning Read-ers." *Language Arts,* 74 (March 1997), 172–184.

Gaskins, I. W., M. A. Downer, R. C. Anderson, P. M. Cun-ningham, R. W. Gaskins, M. Schommer, and The Teach-ers of Benchmark School. "A Metacognitive Approach to Phonics: Using What You Know to Decode What You Don't Know." *Remedial and Special Education* 9 (1988), 36–41.

Gaskins, Irene West, et al. "Procedures for Word Learning: Making Discoveries about Words." *The Reading Teacher,* 50 (December 1996/January 1997), 312–327.

Gaskins, Robert W., Jennifer C. Gaskins, and Irene W. Gaskins. "A Decoding Program for Poor Readers—And the Rest of the Class, Too!" *Language Arts,* 68 (March 1991), 213–225.

Gill, J. Thomas, Jr. "Development of Word Knowledge as It Relates to Reading, Spelling, and Instruction." *Language Arts,* 69 (October 1992), 444–453.

Gipe, Joan P. "Use of a Relevant Context Helps Kids Learn New Word Meanings." *The Reading Teacher,* 33 (January 1980), 398–402.

Glass, Gerald G. "The Strange World of Syllabication." *The Elementary School Journal,* 67 (May 1967), 403–405.

Gough, Philip B. "Word Recognition." In *Handbook of Reading Research,* edited by P. David Pearson et al. New York: Longman, 1984.

Graves, Michael F., and Maureen C. Prenn. "Costs and Benefits of Various Methods of Teaching Vocabulary." *Journal of Reading,* 29 (April 1986), 596–602.

Griffith, Priscilla, and Mary Olson. "Phonemic Awareness Helps Beginning Readers Break the Code." *The Reading Teacher,* 45 (March 1992), 516–523.

Gunning, Thomas G. "Word Building: A Strategic Approach to the Teaching of Phonics." *The Reading Teacher,* 48 (March 1995), 484–488.

Haggard, Martha Rapp. "The Vocabulary Self-Collection Strategy: Using Student Interest and World Knowledge to Enhance Vocabulary Growth." *Journal of Reading,* 29 (April 1986), 634–642.

Hargis, Charles H., et al. "Repetition Requirements for Word Recognition." *Journal of Reading,* 31 (January 1988), 320–327.

Harp, Bill. "Principles of Assessment and Evaluation in Whole Language Classrooms." In *Assessment and Evaluation for Student Centered Learning,* 2d ed., edited by Bill Harp. Norwood, Mass.: Christopher-Gordon, 1994, 47–66.

Heimlich, Joan E., and Susan D. Pittelman. *Semantic Mapping: Classroom Applications.* Newark, Del.: International Reading Association, 1986.

Herman, Patricia A., Richard C. Anderson, P. David Pearson, and William E. Nagy. "Incidental Acquisition of Word Meaning from Expositions with Varied Text Features." *Reading Research Quarterly,* 22, no. 3 (1987), 263–284.

Howell, Helen. "Language, Literature, and Vocabulary Development for Gifted Students." *The Reading Teacher,* 40 (February 1987), 500–504.

HuffBenkoski, Kelly Ann, and Scott C. Greenwood. "The Use of Word Analogy Instruction with Developing Readers." *The Reading Teacher,* 48 (February 1995), 446–447.

Iwicki, Ann L. "Vocabulary Connections." *The Reading Teacher,* 45 (May 1992), 736.

Jenkins, Barbara L., et al. "Children's Use of Hypothesis Testing When Decoding Words." *The Reading Teacher,* 33 (March 1980), 664–667.

Johnson, Dale D., and James F. Baumann. "Word Identification." In *Handbook of Reading Research,* edited by P. David Pearson et al. New York: Longman, 1984.

Johnson, Dale D., Susan D. Pittelman, and Joan E. Heimlich. "Semantic Mapping." *The Reading Teacher,* 39 (April 1986), 778–783.

Johnson, Terry D., and Daphne R. Louis. *Literacy Through Literature.* Portsmouth, N.H.: Heinemann, 1987.

Jolly, Hayden B., Jr. "Teaching Basic Function Words." *The Reading Teacher,* 35 (November 1981), 136–140.

Jones, Linda L. "An Interactive View of Reading: Implications for the Classroom." *The Reading Teacher,* 35 (April 1982), 772–777.

Juel, Connie. "Beginning Reading." In *Handbook of Reading Research, Vol. II,* edited by R. Barr, M. L. Kamil, P. Mosenthal, and P. D. Pearson. New York: Longman, 1991, pp. 759–787.

Juel, Connie. "Learning to Read and Write: A Longitudinal Study of Fifty-four Children from First through Fourth Grade." *Journal of Educational Psychology,* 80 (1988), 437–447.

Kaplan, Elaine M., and Anita Tuchman. "Vocabulary Strategies Belong in the Hands of Learners." *Journal of Reading,* 24 (October 1980), 32–34.

Koeller, Shirley, and Samina Khan. "Going Beyond the Dictionary with the English Vocabulary Explosion." *Journal of Reading,* 24 (April 1981), 628–629.

Koskinen, Patricia S., Robert M. Wilson, Linda B. Gambrell, and Susan B. Neuman. "Captioned Video and Vocabulary Learning: An Innovative Practice in Literacy Instruction." *The Reading Teacher,* 47 (September 1993), 36–43.

Kotrla, Melissa. "What's Literacy?" *The Reading Teacher,* 50, (May 1997), 702–703.

Lapp, Diane, and James Flood. "Where's the Phonics? Making the Case (Again) for Integrated Code Instruction." *The Reading Teacher,* 50 (May 1997), 696–700.

Lundberg, I., J. Frost, and O. Peterson. "Effects of an Extensive Program for Stimulating Phonological Awareness in Preschool Children." *Reading Research Quarterly,* 23 (1988), 263–284.

Maclean, Rod. "Two Paradoxes of Phonics." *The Reading Teacher,* 41 (February 1988), 514–517.

Mangieri, John N., and Michael S. Kahn. "Is the Dolch List of 220 Basic Sight Words Irrelevant?" *The Reading Teacher,* 30 (March 1977), 649–651.

Marzano, Robert J. "A Cluster Approach to Vocabulary Instruction: A New Direction from the Research Literature." *The Reading Teacher,* 38 (November 1984), 168–173.

McConaughy, Stephanie H. "Word Recognition and Word Meaning in the Total Reading Process." *Language Arts,* 55 (November/December 1978), 946–956, 1003.

McGill-Franzen, Anne. "'I Could Read the Words!': Selecting Good Books for Inexperienced Readers." *The Reading Teacher,* 46 (February 1993), 424–426.

McKeown, M. G., I. L. Beck, R. C. Omanson, and C. A. Perfetti. "The Effects of Long-Term Vocabulary Instruction on Reading Comprehension: A Replication." *Journal of Reading Behavior,* 15 (1983), 3–18.

McKeown, Margaret G., Isabel L. Beck, Richard C. Omanson, and Martha T. Pople. "Some Effects of the

Nature and Frequency of Vocabulary Instruction on the Knowledge and Use of Words." *Reading Research Quarterly,* 20, no. 5 (1985), 522–535.

Meltzer, Nancy S., and Robert Herse. "The Boundaries of Written Words as Seen by First Graders." *Journal of Reading Behavior,* 1 (Summer 1969), 3–14.

Morrow, Lesley Mandel, and Diane H. Tracey. "Strategies Used for Phonics Instruction in Early Childhood Classes." *The Reading Teacher,* 50 (May 1997), 644–651.

Nagy, William E. *Teaching Vocabulary to Improve Reading Comprehension.* Urbana, Ill.: National Council of Teachers of English, 1988.

Nagy, William E., and Richard C. Anderson. "How Many Words Are There in Printed School English?" *Reading Research Quarterly,* 19, no. 3 (1984), 304–330.

Nagy, William E., Patricia A. Herman, and Richard C. Anderson. "Learning Words from Context." *Reading Research Quarterly,* 20, no. 2 (1985), 233–253.

Nelson-Herber, Joan. "Expanding and Defining Vocabulary in Content Areas." *Journal of Reading,* 29 (April 1986), 626–633.

Neuman, Susan B., and Patricia S. Koskinen. "Captioned Television as Comprehensible Input: Effects of Incidental Word Learning in Context for Language Minority Students." *Reading Research Quarterly,* 27 (1992), 95–106.

Oleneski, Sue. "Using Jump Rope Rhymes to Teach Reading Skills." *The Reading Teacher,* 46 (October 1992), 173–175.

Palmer, Barbara. "Dolch List Still Useful." *The Reading Teacher,* 38 (March 1985), 708–709.

Pearson, P. David. "Focus on Research: Teaching and Learning Reading: A Research Perspective." *Language Arts,* 70 (October 1993), 502–511.

Peterson, Susan, and Patricia H. Phelps. "Visual-Auditory Links: A Structural Analysis Approach to Increase Word Power." *The Reading Teacher,* 44 (March 1991), 524–525.

Petrick, Pamela Bondi. "Creative Vocabulary Instruction in the Content Area." *Journal of Reading,* 35 (March 1992), 481–482.

Pettersen, Nancy-Laurel. "Grate/Great Homonym Hunt." *Journal of Reading,* 31 (January 1988), 374–375.

Pigg, John R. "The Effects of a Storytelling/Storyreading Program on the Language Skills of Rural Primary Students." Unpublished paper. Cookeville, Tenn.: Tennessee Technological University, 1986.

Powell, William R. "Teaching Vocabulary Through Opposition." *Journal of Reading,* 29 (April 1986), 617–621.

Readence, John E., R. Scott Baldwin, and Martha H. Head. "Direct Instruction in Processing Metaphors." *Journal of Reading Behavior,* 18, no. 4 (1986), 325–339.

Readence, John E., R. Scott Baldwin, and Martha H. Head. "Teaching Young Readers to Interpret Metaphors." *The Reading Teacher,* 40 (January 1987), 439–443.

Readence, John E., R. Scott Baldwin, Robert J. Rickelman, and G. Michael Miller. "The Effect of Vocabulary Instruction on Interpreting Metaphor." In *Solving Problems in Literacy: Learners, Teachers, and Researchers,* edited by Jerome A. Niles and Rosary V. Lalik. Rochester, N.Y.: National Reading Conference, 1986.

Richek, Margaret Ann. "Relating Vocabulary Learning to World Knowledge." *Journal of Reading,* 32 (December 1988), 262–267.

Richgels, Donald, Karla Poremba, and Lea M. McGee. "Kindergartners Talk about Print: Phonemic Awareness in Meaningful Contexts." *The Reading Teacher,* 49 (May 1996), 632–642.

Richler, Howard. "Word Play: You're Likely to Be Clipped." *Notes Plus* (March 1996), 11–12.

Roe, Betty D. *Use of Storytelling/Storyreading in Conjunction with Follow-up Language Activities to Improve Oral Communication of Rural First Grade Students: Phase I.* Cookeville, Tenn.: Rural Education Consortium, 1985.

Roe, Betty D. *Use of Storytelling/Storyreading in Conjunction with Follow-up Language Activities to Improve Oral Communication of Rural Primary Grade Students: Phase II.* Cookeville, Tenn.: Rural Education Consortium, 1986.

Roser, N., and C. Juel. "Effects of Vocabulary Instruction on Reading Comprehension." In *New Inquiries in Reading Research and Instruction,* Thirty-First Yearbook of the National Reading Conference, edited by J. A. Niles and L. A. Harris. Rochester, N.Y.: National Reading Conference, 1982.

Rosso, Barbara Rak, and Robert Emans. "Children's Use of Phonic Generalizations." *The Reading Teacher,* 34 (March 1981), 653–657.

Ruddiman, Joan. "The Vocab Game: Empowering Students Through Word Awareness." *Journal of Reading,* 36 (February 1993), 400–401.

Saccardi, Marianne. "Predictable Books: Gateways to a Lifetime of Reading." *The Reading Teacher,* 49 (April 1996), 588–590.

Samuels, S. Jay. "Decoding and Automaticity: Helping Poor Readers Become Automatic at Word Recognition." *The Reading Teacher,* 41 (April 1988), 756–760.

Schatz, Elinore K., and R. Scott Baldwin. "Context Clues Are Unreliable Predictors of Word Meanings." *Reading Research Quarterly,* 21, no. 4 (1986), 439–453.

Schell, Leo M. "Teaching Decoding to Remedial Readers." *Journal of Reading,* 31 (May 1978), 877–882.

Schwartz, Robert M. "Learning to Learn Vocabulary in Content Area Textbooks." *Journal of Reading,* 32 (November 1988), 108–118.

Schwartz, Robert M., and Taffy E. Raphael. "Concept of Definition: A Key to Improving Students' Vocabulary." *The Reading Teacher,* 39 (November 1985), 198–205.

Sippola, Arne E. "What to Teach for Reading Readiness—A Research Review and Materials Inventory." *The Reading Teacher,* 39 (November 1985), 162–167.

Smith, Carl B. "Vocabulary Development in Content Area Reading." *The Reading Teacher,* 43 (March 1990), 508–509.

Spiegel, Dixie Lee. "Reinforcement in Phonics Materials." *The Reading Teacher,* 43 (January 1990), 328–329.

Stahl, Steven A. "Saying the 'P' Word: Nine Guidelines for Exemplary Phonics Instruction." *The Reading Teacher,* 45 (April 1992), 618–625.

Stahl, Steven A. "Three Principles of Effective Vocabulary Instruction." *Journal of Reading,* 29 (April 1986), 662–668.

Stahl, Steven A., Jean Osborn, and Fran Lehr. *Beginning to Read: Thinking and Learning about Print—A Summary.* Champaign, Ill.: University of Illinois, Center for the Study of Reading, 1990.

Stahl, Steven A., and Sandra J. Vancil. "Discussion Is What Makes Semantic Maps Work in Vocabulary Instruction." *The Reading Teacher,* 40 (October 1986), 62–67.

"A Talk with Marilyn Adams." *Language Arts,* 68 (March 1991), 206–212.

Taylor, Barbara M., and Linda Nosbush. "Oral Reading for Meaning: A Technique for Word Identification." *The Reading Teacher,* 37 (December 1983), 234–237.

Thelen, Judith N. "Vocabulary Instruction and Meaningful Learning." *Journal of Reading,* 29 (April 1986), 603–609.

Thompson, Stephen J. "Teaching Metaphoric Language: An Instructional Strategy." *Journal of Reading,* 30 (November 1986), 105–109.

Tovey, Duane R. "Children's Grasp of Phonics Terms vs. Sound-Symbol Relationships." *The Reading Teacher,* 33 (January 1980), 431–437.

Trachtenburg, Phyllis. "Using Children's Literature to Enhance Phonics Instruction." *The Reading Teacher,* 43 (May 1990), 648–654.

Veatch, Jeanette. "From the Vantage of Retirement." *The Reading Teacher,* 49 (1996), 510–516.

Waugh, R. P., and K. W. Howell. "Teaching Modern Syllabication." *The Reading Teacher,* 29 (October 1975), 20–25.

White, Thomas G., Joanne Sowell, and Alice Yanagihara. "Teaching Elementary Students to Use Word-Part Clues." *The Reading Teacher,* 42 (January 1989), 302–308.

Yopp, Hallie. "Read-Aloud Books for Developing Phonemic Awareness: An Annotated Bibliography." *The Reading Teacher,* 48 (March 1995), 538–542.

Yopp, Hallie Kay. "Developing Phonemic Awareness in Young Children." *The Reading Teacher,* 45 (May 1992), 696–703.

Yopp, Hallie Kay. "A Test for Assessing Phonemic Awareness in Young Children." *The Reading Teacher,* 49 (September 1995), 20–29.

If you would like to examine this primer's parent text:

Teaching Reading in Today's Elementary Schools

Seventh Edition
Burns/Roe/Ross © 1999
(title code: 3-07855   ISBN: 0-395-903475)

please contact our Faculty Service Center at

Houghton Mifflin Company
2075 Foxfield Road, Suite 100
St. Charles, IL 60174
1-800-733-1717   FAX 1-800-733-1810

http://www.hmco.com/college

BRIEF CONTENTS

Teaching Reading in Today's Elementary Schools